TRAPPED

TRAPPED

HOW THE WORLD RESCUED 33 MINERS FROM 2,000 FEET BELOW THE CHILEAN DESERT

MARC ARONSON

Atheneum Books for Young Readers
NEW YORK LONDON TORONTO SYDNEY NEW DELHI

ATHENEUM BOOKS FOR YOUNG READERS
An imprint of Simon & Schuster Children's Publishing Division
1230 Avenue of the Americas, New York, New York 10020
Text copyright © 2011 by Marc Aronson
Cover photographs courtesy of AP Photo/Dario Lopez-Mills
All rights reserved, including the right of reproduction in whole or in part in any form.
ATHENEUM BOOKS FOR YOUNG READERS is a registered trademark of Simon & Schuster, Inc.
Atheneum logo is a trademark of Simon & Schuster, Inc.
For information about special discounts for bulk purchases, please contact Simon & Schuster
Special Sales at 1-866-506-1949 or business@simonandschuster.com.
The Simon & Schuster Speakers Bureau can bring authors to your live event. For more
information or to book an event, contact the Simon & Schuster Speakers Bureau at
1-866-248-3049 or visit our website at www.simonspeakers.com.
Also available in an Atheneum Books for Young Readers hardcover edition
A Book by Aronson & Glenn LLC
Produced by Marc Aronson and John W. Glenn
Book design, production, and illustrations by Jon Glick, mouse+tiger
The text for this book was set in Bembo.
Manufactured in the United States of America
0821 OFF
First Atheneum Books for Young Readers paperback edition March 2019
10 9 8 7 6 5 4
The Library of Congress has catalogued the hardcover edition as follows:
Aronson, Marc.
Trapped : how the world rescued 33 miners from 2,000 feet below the Chilean desert /
Marc Aronson. — 1st ed.
p. cm.
Includes bibliographical references and index.
ISBN 978-1-4169-1397-9 (hardback)
1. Mine accidents—Chile—Copiapó Region—Juvenile literature. 2. Mine rescue work—
Chile—Copiapó Region—Juvenile literature. 3. Copper mines and mining—Accidents—
Chile—Copiapó Region—Juvenile literature. 4. Copper mines and mining—Accidents—
Chile—Copiapó Region—Juvenile literature. I. Title.
TN311.A76 2011 363.11'96223430983145—dc22 2011000777
ISBN 978-1-4424-4025-8 (pbk)
ISBN 978-1-4424-3981-8 (eBook)

Photography and Illustrations Credits

Interior, pages x–1, 6: Jon Glick, mouse+tiger; 7: courtesy NASA; 9: Jon Glick, mouse+tiger; 10:
courtesy Diavik Diamond Mines, Inc.; 12: courtesy of West Virginia Office of Miners' Health Safety
and Training Map Archives; 15: courtesy Kelvin Brown/Reflex Instruments; 18: The George F.
Landegger Collection of Alabama Photographs in Carol M. Highsmith's America, Library of Congress,
Prints and Photographs Division; 19: from *De Re Metallica* (1556); 23: Jon Glick, mouse+tiger; 30:
courtesy Kelvin Brown/Reflex Instruments; 33 (*both*): courtesy Kelvin Brown/Reflex Instruments;
35: courtesy of Marios Philippides; 39, 41: courtesy Kelvin Brown/Reflex Instruments; 47: AP Photo/
Hector Retamal; 48–49, 52: courtesy Kelvin Brown/Reflex Instruments; 53: Jon Glick, mouse+tiger;
55 (*both*): courtesy NASA; 59: courtesy Kelvin Brown/Reflex Instruments; 63, 67: courtesy NASA; 69:
Jon Glick, mouse+tiger; 73: courtesy Kelvin Brown/Reflex Instruments; 77: Jon Glick, mouse+tiger;
79: courtesy of Center Rock, Inc.; 80: AP Photo/Chile's Government Video; 85: courtesy of Center
Rock, Inc.; 88: Jon Glick, mouse+tiger; 89, 90, 91: AP Photo/Hugo Infante, Chilean government

Insert, page 1: courtesy Kelvin Brown/Reflex Instruments; 2 (*both*): courtesy NASA; 3–4: courtesy
Kelvin Brown/Reflex Instruments; 5 (*top*): courtesy NASA; 5 (*bottom*): courtesy Kelvin Brown/Reflex
Instruments; 6: courtesy of Center Rock, Inc.; 7: AP Photo/Chile's Government Video; 8: AP Photo/
Hugo Infante, Chilean government

CONTENTS

TRAPPED

PART ONE

COPIAPÓ, CHILE:
ABOVE
BELOW

AUGUST 5–22, 2010

CHAPTER ONE

AUGUST 5-6

2:00 PM

Raul Villegas was driving a truck up a ramp . . . 1,800 feet underground . . . when he heard the crack and first saw the dust. Villegas was used to hauling rock out of copper mines in northern Chile, so he had often heard the creaks and moans of the angry earth. He drove on, passing a couple of miners heading down. But as he inched up the ramp he felt a wave hit his truck, "like when there is a dynamite explosion." Glancing back, it was as if he were looking down the heart of an erupting volcano. He rushed up the endless, sharp turns of the corkscrewing mine and finally made it to the surface. He, at least, was safe. But when he described the sound and dust cloud to his bosses, no one listened.

Someone told Villegas to drive back down, into the mine.

This time he could only go so far. Some 1,200 feet down there was no longer a road, and all around him he could hear the sounds of groaning rock. He turned around and sped up, out of the darkness. Something was very wrong in the San José Mine.

9:00 PM

Six men trained to handle mine emergencies retraced the route of Villegas's truck, daring to go down to see what had happened, to find whoever was trapped in the mine.

6:00 AM

The exhausted rescue crew returned . . . alone.

So began one part of a story that captured the attention of the world—bringing together everyone, from experts on outer space to drill bit manufacturers from Pennsylvania, from nutritionists to camera crews. But the real story started millions of years earlier.

CHAPTER TWO

OF EARTH AND COLD

FORTY MILLION YEARS AGO the great dance of the shifting continents took on a new rhythm—one that still carries us along today. In the age of the dinosaurs, the Earth was relatively hotter than it is now. But then the Indian subcontinent slammed into the rest of Asia, pushing up the Himalayas. The great wall of mountains served as a kind of air rudder, bending winds and creating new weather patterns that defined where and how animals, plants, and—much later—people could live throughout Asia and beyond. According to some scientists, the rising jagged peaks altered the entire planet in still another way. In the hot, humid ages, our atmosphere had more carbon dioxide in it than it does now. That particular gas is easily absorbed by certain rocks—the very ones that were uplifted and exposed to the air by the rising mountains. The more carbon dioxide that was pulled from the air by the fingers of the Himalayas, the more temperatures dropped all over the Earth.

One reason to believe this theory is that the Himalayas thrust up at the same time ice caps began to form at the poles of Earth. Quite possibly, if there were no Mount Everest, the Antarctic would not be covered in snow and ice. One part of the great dance was the crunching grind of the Himalayas into the air, and the cooling around the whole world. The other dance partner was formed out of the same process.

As the ice caps at the poles grew, icy currents spread through the seas. One such cold stream is called the Humbolt Current, and thirteen million years ago it began rushing up from the Antarctic along the Pacific coast of South America. Frigid water in the ocean means fewer clouds, less rain. And so, along that particular coast, the land turned extremely dry. In what is called the Atacama Desert it may not rain for three years, five years, even fifty years. We think of Death Valley as dry, but plants grow there. In the Atacama there is just bare rock—except in that rare moment when the rains come and the ground blushes purple with life.

The cold water and dry land had one more strange effect. Just along the Pacific coast of South America, the crust of our earth slides. A gigantic formation called the Nazca Plate, which stretches all the way to the middle of the Pacific Ocean, hits up against the coast of the continent, and then dips down. If you looked beneath the mountains and valleys, the rivers and plains, you would see what looks like an immense down escalator, as the Nazca Plate slips under the continent. Because the land along the coast is so dry, there are no rivers slowly taking soil out to sea, so the plate has no coating of soft ground to serve as a kind of grease to allow it to easily slip under the rock. Instead, the plate bangs hard and strong against the

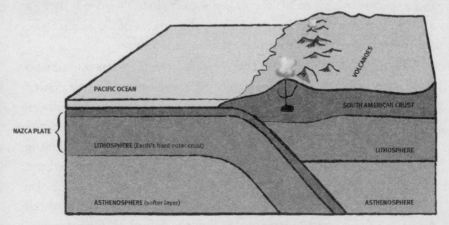

This simplified diagram shows how the Nazca Plate bangs into and slides under the continent of South America.

The long straight line of the Atacama Fault is so distinct it is clearly visible from space.

continent, forcing up the tall peaks of the Andes. The mountains, in turn, block any bits of rain that might be heading for the coast.

Looking down at the coast of South America from space, there is a long, straight line in the earth. This is the very old Atacama Fault—a direct result of the pressure of the Nazca Plate. All along this fault line there are erupting volcanoes and earthquakes as the plate pushes down, slams into the continent, and forces the mountains up higher. The Andes, according to this theory, then became the dance partner of the Himalayas, and together they set the tune for our cold age.

Today, in the dry, brown desert of Chile, where no animals and plants can live, the much older, deeper form of movement and change continues. The earth cracks, splinters, splays, and deep veins running along the immense fault lines are exposed. In those crevices, our planet gives up its treasures: gold, silver, and copper. If we were honest we would not name the Americas after Amerigo Vespucci, the Italian mapmaker and navigator. Instead, we'd properly name the two continents Potosí, for it was the hill of silver found in the town of Potosí in what is now Bolivia by the Spanish in the 1500s—and still mined today—that truly made the New World matter. The flood of silver from that mine linked together trade all over the world. And if we were similarly fair, we'd rename the nation of Chile as Copper. For nearly a hundred years, the story of Chile has been the story of copper—the treasure of the deep desert. It takes just one thing to bring out that treasure: men. Men willing to go out into the heat, and down into the mines.

DOWN

"A hundred feet down is no different from a thousand feet—a total absence of light." That's what the former miner and geologist Ron Mishkin tells me as we enter the adit of the Sterling Hill Mine Museum in Ogdensburg, New Jersey. As he explains it, using a whole dictionary of old mining terms, when Sterling Hill was an active zinc mine, men walked into "the dry [a locker room], changed into their ratty mine clothes, got their protective gear, brassed in [checked in, with a brass nameplate], and entered the adit portal. They walked to the lamp room where they put the Edison cap lamp [a personal lightbulb] on their hard hat and the heavy battery plus the self-rescuer unit [allows miners to breathe in the presence of poison gas] on their safety belt. The miners then headed to the man cage in the shaft." In an amusement park, the man cage might be the one ride you wouldn't take. The cage looks like a giant roller-coaster car and holds about thirty men—three abreast in each of ten inclined benches. There are no seat belts. When ready to descend down the shaft, the station attendant rings the code and the hoist engineer sends the cage down the shaft into the pitch black at one thousand feet per minute. And now it

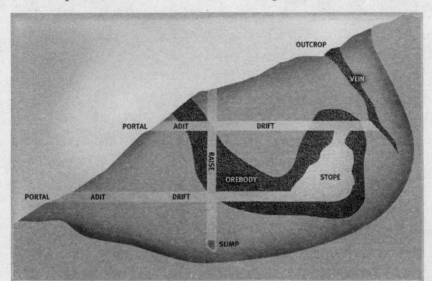

THE LANGUAGE OF THE MINES

PORTAL: entrance

ADIT: from Latin for "access," a straight or horizontal pathway into a mine

DRIFT: a horizontal pathway within a mine that follows a vein of ore

RAISE: a vertical or inclined shaft in a mine created by digging up from a lower level; the same shift carved downward is called a "winze."

SUMP: the lowest point in a mine; may be used to collect water drained from other areas

OREBODY: the mineral or metal being mined

OUTCROP: desired ore visible from the surface

STOPE: the area emptied out as ore is removed

The Diavik Diamond Mine in Canada. Open pit mines such as this show our capacity to gouge out the earth.

is dark. Not dark like midnight, or a home with the lights off, or even a street during a power outage. It is black, as if there were no sun, stars, moon. No airplanes, candles, or distant headlights. Dark so deep that every miner knows he must work with a buddy, because if your hard-hat light goes out all you have is the feel of the rock. There are no directions, no guides, just black. In mine museums, the pathways are illuminated—not in working mines. The miner has the lamp on his hard hat; he can see straight in front of him, that's it.

In recent years, "down" has come to mean, "really far down." The deepest mines in the world are the TauTona and Savuka gold mines in South Africa, which are working at depths close to 12,800 feet. Ron Mishkin says that at that depth, temperatures can reach 113 degrees, and it requires massive refrigeration units even to "cool" the working area to a mere 82 degrees. After 5,280 feet (a mile), the cable holding the elevator car gets so heavy, it will soon crack under its own weight. So miners must descend one mile straight down, only to change elevators and fall yet another mile. Ron says the drop is one of the most frightening parts of being a miner. As you go down you realize how far you are from sunlight and safety—how cut off you would be if anything went wrong. Once you stop dropping you are no longer thinking about the earth you have left behind. You are somewhere else, in a totally different kingdom. You work, you forget, you have other challenges.

The darkness of a mine seems to have its own weight. Or maybe that is just the dawning sense you have of where you are. If you think of a mine as a place where men with pickaxes fleck stones one at a time off of the inner face of the earth, you are missing the force that is most useful to miners: gravity. Miners try to use weight to their advantage. Teams carefully drill and blast gaps in the rock in a way that the mineral or metal they seek, mixed with whatever holds it, will cascade down into a convenient pile, where it can be carted off to be sorted, processed, and separated. Miners use explosives to put endless rivers of stone in motion—right above their heads. When Onofre Tafoya began his first day digging for copper at the San Manuel Copper Mine in Arizona, he suddenly realized that "1,415 feet of earth above me was in motion like a fluid, crushing itself as it flowed down." The miner dares to set loose a current of rock.

A mine is a kind of immense mural revealing millions of years of history. You may see white limestone—once the bottom of a sea, now slanted upward from when the earth, like a waking giant, rose from its watery bed. At Sterling Hill, the angled white may be interrupted by a huge bubble of black—blobs that were once magma rushing out of volcanoes, but then were cooled and formed into igneous rocks until they sunk down, like heavy tear drops through the softer limestone. Walking through a mine is like touring an aquarium, but instead of water, fish, and plants behind glass, you see the swirling traces of the liquid earth, the true history of our planet. Miners must read that history to discover its secrets.

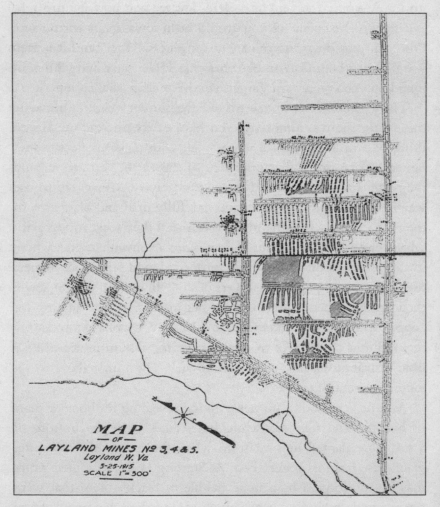

MAP
— OF —
LAYLAND MINES Nº 3, 4 & 5.
Layland W. Va.
5-25-1915
SCALE 1"= 500'

This mine map from West Virginia is nearly a century old, but diagramming the exact location of tunnels and shafts is just as important today.

But unlike scholars on the surface, they cannot record their nuggets of wisdom in well-lit libraries. Instead they have to hack them out in the total darkness. That is only possible because of planning.

A mine is not a ditch, it is a plan. Before men go in they have to know where the vein of metal is located and how it runs. Each hidden river runs its own course, which demands its own attack. You can dig down to ore or you can dig up. You can hit it from the side or aslant. But someone has to hold that map and fill in each blank space as men return and report. The map is like a superhero's X-ray vision—it shows people on the surface what is going on inside the earth. Without a good map, the men underground might as well be on the moon.

Chile has some large, efficient, and very modern mines with terrific maps and the very latest equipment to monitor and protect miners. When Dr. William Chavez brings college students from the United States to see those mines, they are "astonished." They leave home imagining that Chile will be slow and backward. Then they see operations that would be the envy of any in the United States or Canada. But there are also some much smaller mines that are like an attic—people sort of know where everything is, and don't really know where anything is. Why would anyone risk going into a pitch-black space that isn't safe? The answer lies in the shacks near Copiapó.

CHAPTER THREE

THE MEN OF HEPHAISTOS

COPIAPÓ

Two thousand ten was a lucky year in Copiapó, the small capital of the Atacama region of Chile: For the first time in recent memory, it rained. Suddenly the town plaza burst into bloom.

According to Clive Maund, an Englishman who has long lived in Chile, around the plaza teenagers rush by on skateboards, musicians play, and men who are not needed in the mines rest and wait for their next job. "Copiapó" means "crucible of gold"—a container that allows gold to be heated and refined—and the town owes its existence to the nearby gold and copper mines. The Candelaria mine, near Copiapó, even inspired two festivals in the town. For in 1780, one Mariano Caro Inca is said to have found a statue of the Virgin Mary holding the baby Jesus when he ducked away from a storm into a rock shelter. There is now a chapel in town dedicated to the Virgin of the Candelaria, as well as two festivals in her honor. But while mines need workers and offer relatively good hourly wages, many of the men in the plaza are struggling.

Outside the town are neighborhoods, such as Padre Negro, filled with shacks where miners and their families live. The reporters Franklin Briceno and Eva Vergara captured the scene this way: "On a clear night, the glittering streetlights of Copiapó stretch out like a beautiful carpet below mountains that hold the promise of copper and gold. But Padre Negro's thirty-eight houses lack access to sewers and running water." Anyone living there has to walk several blocks to collect water from a public tap, then carry it home.

The dry desert hills near the San José Mine. The Atacama Desert may not see rainfall for decades, which creates this lifeless, almost lunar, landscape.

In some of these tough districts, local gangs mark off their turf by tying sneakers to poles. So when the mines are hiring, the men of Copiapó leave the town and disappear into the desert. Out in the brown dunes there are many small and medium-sized pits where a man can get work if he doesn't ask too many questions. One of these mines is called San José.

San José is an old digging, started in 1889, which spirals down to around 2,400 feet. As Dr. Chavez explains, "mines never die." Even when a mine seems tapped out, someone will come along with a new plan, a new idea of where and how to look. And when the world wants copper, there is always a good reason to give an old hole a new look.

The first half of the San José was dug in the early twentieth century, and the mine has not been well maintained. The digging was even shut down in 2007 after a geologist's assistant was killed in an explosion. But as copper prices rose the following year, it reopened. Mine owners were eager to get what they could out of the earth, and miners in Copiapó were just as glad to have a chance to work. They set out to San José, even as word came that something was not right in the mine.

The men who were trapped in the mine knew they were taking a big risk by going down into San José. And if they tried to ignore the danger, their families spoke up reminding them. For example, Richard Vega's father was an experienced miner and kept telling him, "Son, that mine is sending you a warning, stop working there." "Dad," Richard answered, "I'm fixing up my house, I need to carry on." Lilianett Gómez's husband, Mario, had even protested to the owners about the conditions in the mine. But she later told a reporter, "The bosses said, 'If you don't want to work in the mine, then get up and go. There are four or five others who will happily take your place.'" A miner works where there is work.

The hope of making a bit of money draws men from places like Padre Negro out into the desert and then down into the San José Mine. But what makes copper valuable? Why do we turn ourselves into moles burrowing down into the earth in search of it? The answer to that lies in the magic at the beginning of civilization.

COPPER

When we think of magic it is easy to picture Merlin or some other wizard chanting spells or concocting potions. Or if you shift from story to history, there were the alchemists whose experiments J. K. Rowling studied as she wrote the Harry Potter books. But there is an older magic, a real magic, we too easily forget. This story is like one of those powerful dreams that come just before you wake up—you are haunted by the images that crossed your mind, even if you can't quite recall them. I'm speaking about the magic of the metalsmiths.

As far back as the 6000s BC people had figured out that they could find bits of loose copper and work with them—either by banging or heating. Cooper looks nice and can be shaped, but it is not strong—it makes better decoration than weapons. But in many ancient myths, just as in modern fantasy novels, there comes a moment where a god or hero is about to begin a quest, and needs a special weapon. To obtain that magic sword and shield, that helmet and armor, that chariot and bridle, he goes to the god of the forge— the master of metal and fire. The Greeks called him Hephaistos, the Romans named him Vulcan. The blacksmith god creates the tool the hero needs, and yet he is lame and ugly, a figure of fun. Even in India, the Hindu god of fire, Agni, has no feet.

Most recently, in Rick Riordan's *The Lightning Thief,* Percy and Annabeth are almost trapped in a Tunnel of Love amusement park ride. When they go to confront Ares for setting them up, he snorts, "Bet that crippled blacksmith was surprised when he netted a couple of stupid kids." Indeed, in the original Greek myth, Hephaistos does catch his beautiful wife, Aphrodite, dating his own disloyal brother Ares. But when the snared lovers are brought before the gods, the Olympians laugh—at Hephaistos. Why is that? Why is the divine creator who makes the tools heroes need always off to the side—a required stop on the way, but never a true hero himself?

Hephaistos is occasionally honored as the master of the forge, as shown in this 1904 statue. In most myths, however, he is treated as ugly and often a figure of fun.

The great moment of the masters of the forge came in the 2000s BC. For someone, somewhere, somehow figured out that if you took a certain kind of black sand (we now know it as tin) and mixed it with copper—in just the right ratio of one part tin to eight-to-ten parts copper—you would create bronze. Bronze was the sacred metal; it created the sword that would not bend, the shield that would not break, the bridle no horse could resist, the container that would hold all treasures.

Some say that men who could not fight learned to work with metal—so perhaps many smiths were indeed lame. Others think that blacksmiths heated metals containing arsenic, which gave off acrid, poisonous fumes—so perhaps they were disfigured. And surely sparks and flames must have burned many a hand and foot. And yet I suspect there is something else in our stories of the smith who is both needed for his skills and as the subject of jokes. At one time making bronze must have seemed both mysterious and magical. The inventor of bronze must have seemed to have tamed fire, to have shaped earth, to have given human beings both a gift

This illustration from *De Re Metallica*, the great book on mining and metalwork first published in the 1500s, shows workers using fire to melt ore. The book was translated into English by future president Herbert Hoover and his wife, Lou Henry Hoover.

of the gods and the tools of envy, war, and conflict. He must have seemed necessary and dangerous.

Bronze spread remarkably quickly across what is now Turkey, Greece, and then the rest of Europe and on to China. In just five hundred years, groups of people that had no common language shared the one secret everyone needed to know. Yet once warriors had their weapons, they mocked the master of the forge, the inventor of bronze. They called him lame and ugly, a mere worker with rough hands, not a shining hero. And in a way we still do that today—we eagerly use the treasures of the deep earth that miners bring us, while ignoring the men in the mines.

Eventually iron, and then steel, took the place of copper and bronze. But then, at the end of the 1800s, the world went electric. First telegraphs, then telephones—talk ran on copper wires. Just at the moment when the world suddenly needed more copper, a new process was invented that made it easier to separate the metal from other rocks. So even as metalsmiths crafted the Bronze Age, coppersmiths made possible the Age of Electricity. Today, the average American uses sixteen pounds of copper a year—at home, at work, and at school. Five pounds of that is recycled, but that means for every American, eleven new pounds of copper must be found, mined, processed, and shipped.

On the coast of Chile, the deep time of the Nazca Plate and the Atacama Fault meets the very modern need for copper. And so the men of Copiapó were called to descend the spiraling ramps of the San José Mine.

CHAPTER FOUR

AUGUST 5–8: "MURDERERS"

AUGUST 6 ABOVE GATHERING

The rescue crew brought back no clues about the men down in the mine. The only official word was a bulletin as cold and silent as rock, "the assessment of the terrain indicates that there is a blockage in the mine's main shaft." Still, family, friends, relatives, and other miners rushed to the site—as if being near the hole in the earth would bring them closer to the missing men. Workmen came carrying shovels, wishing, dreaming that they could move mountains and save their neighbors. They were scared, angry, and holding on to one last emotion like a precious lifeline: hope. "We hope they are all fine," a relative of one of the miners told a reporter, "but we are also angry because we have no information."

Ximena Matas, the governor of the Atacama region, finally spelled out exactly what was known: At least thirty-four men were missing (that was later corrected to thirty-three). They were about nine hundred feet underground, which meant some four and half miles of winding road corkscrewed down to them, and it was entirely blocked by the seven hundred thousand tons of rock that had fallen down. No one was sure why the cascade of rocks had sealed off the mine—whether men were given poor directions and blasted off rocks that should never have been touched, setting off the avalanche, or if the earth moved on its own. But that was not the question. Causes could wait, for the moment all anyone could think about were the consequences: the men trapped in the mine. The one possible piece of good news was that there was a space set aside as a refuge in the area below the collapse. As Matas explained, "There is a shelter with the basics needed to support people for a time, such as oxygen, protective gear, overcoats." If the men were alive, and if they managed to reach that space, they would be able to survive . . . for perhaps a few days. Many, many ifs. And even if they were in the shelter, how could they get out?

AUGUST 7 **ABOVE** FAILURE

Overnight, a bonfire became a home in the desert. The anxious people huddled together around the flame, worrying, wondering. No one was leaving the mine, even if there was nothing anyone could do but wait. But wheels were turning. The newly elected president of Chile arrived and "personally promised the families of the trapped miners the rescue operations will continue with all the strength in the world." Indeed, Laurence Golborne, the nation's top minister of mining, was at San José taking charge.

Two days earlier San José was a mine out of sight, ignored, nothing like the vast operations that so impressed Dr. Chavez's students. In America, mines are required to have two escape routes, and they must be at least five hundred feet apart so that if one is blocked, the other may still be clear. Chile has similar rules and they are carefully enforced—in the big mines. San José did not have, and never had, a single escape route. It did not matter enough to anyone to make sure it did. "It was always a dangerous place to work," a miner recalled, "all of us who went in there would wonder, 'will we make it out?'" But as reporters started to arrive at the disaster site, Chile's leadership knew it must act. The new president was elected on the promise of promoting business—he needed to make sure the whole world saw Chile as the home of those clean, modern mines. The country's reputation as a center of good mining practice now rested on the fate of thirty-three men,

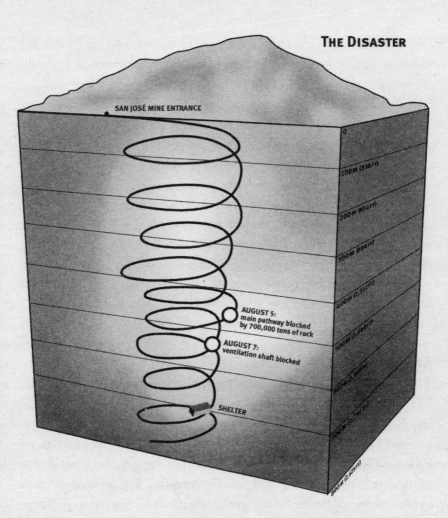

SAN JOSÉ MINE ENTRANCE

0

100 M (338 ft)

200 M (656 ft)

300 M (984 ft)

400 M (1,312 ft)

500 M (1,640 ft)

600 M (1,968 ft)

700 M (2,296 ft)

800 M (2,624 ft)

AUGUST 5:
main pathway blocked
by 700,000 tons of rock

AUGUST 7:
ventilation shaft blocked

SHELTER

who had disappeared, eaten by the rock, the mine, the silence. Something had to happen, fast.

The main road down was sealed shut, but there was one other path: an air shaft. Could enough rock be cleared from it to send trucks rumbling down to the men? By now more than 130 rescue workers had reached San José—enough bodies and equipment, if the mine was stable. Crews started down the shaft, but rocks began falling again. Men scampered back up to safety. The earth was not done moving. Neither the main entrance nor the air shaft was safe.

AUGUST 8 ABOVE TEARS IN THE NIGHT

The bonfire blazed again, holding the families together through the night. Now there were some chairs, blankets, a single tent going up. But news of a second collapse seemed like a death sentence for the relatives. Reporters heard anguished wailing. Later in the day some men ran to the mine, as if they could battle their way down themselves. "Murderers!" they shouted at officers from the mine. Even Minister Golborne was shaken. As Alonso Soto reported for Reuters, Golborne, "his voice cracking," admitted that "the easiest, most logical way in is now blocked. Experts are going to have to find other alternatives, but those will be tougher and take longer."

Where could Golborne find the very best "experts"?

ABOVE THE LIEUTENANT

The deepest underground copper mine in the world is El Teniente, "The Lieutenant." It is high on a hill in Chile, but it is nothing like San José. At one time the home to some 16,000 people, it had its own hospital, its own train line, and is now owned and run by CODELCO, which is actually a division of the government. Andre Sougarret, an engineer, and René Aguilar, a risk management expert, were sent from El Teniente to bring their special knowledge to the Atacama Desert. And they were not alone. People were flying in to Chile from around the world to help. But too many hands are almost as bad as too few—the helpers needed a plan.

AUGUST 5–7 BELOW FACING THE TRUTH

Victor Segovia was on his way up, out of the mine when he "saw rocks falling down and there was no way of escape." Dust was blowing everywhere, getting in the miners' eyes, temporarily blinding some and leaving the others blinking back tears. Hundreds of thousands of tons of falling rock sent a blast of air through the mine that made Yonni Barrios feel like his ears were "being sucked from one side to the other." Segovia turned and ran away from the light, into the darkness.

Three men quickly took roles as leaders. Mario Gómez, the eldest; the irrepressible Mario Sepúlveda, a big, spirited miner, known for his jokes and sense of humor, who seemed to find new strength in the crisis; and Luis Urzúa, the shift foreman.

Urzúa looks like an old-time catcher on a baseball team— that round, thick, solid guy who gets nicked and knocked by the stinging foul tips, the blazing fastballs, and the sliding spikes but is the backstop holding the team together. He is a veteran miner who was known to be "very protective of his people." In that terrifying moment, most of the men trusted him. They knew that Urzúa was not only a good man but savvy and careful. "We always say," he explained later, "that when you go into the mine you respect the mine and hope you get out." Respect is the key to survival underground. Even the most careful miner cannot stop rock from falling, but he can improve his odds so long as the earth behaves. Ron Mishkin shakes his head sadly when he says, "every accident that I've seen came from someone being foolish." Most of the men were trained; they knew there was just one safe place. "The only thing we could do was run down into a shelter—which saved us from certain death."

Urzúa gathered men and gave them assignments. One crew got in a truck and drove up, seeing how far they could go. But there was so much dust in the air, they couldn't see the road and crashed. Not good, yet Urzúa quickly realized that even the accident brought useful knowledge: They could not go up, so all their attention would have to be on surviving below. Some of the men were talking about being stuck for a couple of days. But when Urzúa saw the rock and the dust, he "knew otherwise."

The good news: The men were alive, together, in the shelter.

The bad news: They were isolated, in darkness so complete they could not even see one another, they could only make out the sounds of other frightened voices, with no way to tell the outside world where they were or that they were alive. They were buried beneath the rock; breathing, but buried. Since they were near underground magma streams, it was seriously hot—ninety-degree temperatures with 90 percent humidity. All Segovia could think about was "to let my family know I was alive, but there was no way of doing it. Many times I lost hope."

Hope—it is such a frail word. Hope offers nothing concrete, no plan, no schedule, just a wish, a prayer, a belief—it flickers on, and then flickers off. And when it goes, the blank darkness, the icy silence is easily filled with rage—that is what was happening around the bonfire above ground. The same was true deep inside the mine. Some of the miners were sure they were lost, that they would starve. "We were waiting for death," Richard Villarroel admitted.

In the black air anger flared.

Already there were splits—five of the miners were not part of Urzúa's crew; they insisted on tunneling back up. There was an air shaft nearby, but the ladder to it was too short, and then a boulder sealed it shut. And some miners say there was a third group, which stood against both Urzúa and the five. Fist fights were breaking out—after all, you can hit a guy you don't like even if you can't make a dent in the rock.

Urzúa did not have time for fights. His concerns were food and water, then waste. He had to figure out how to meet their most basic needs. But that also created a great opportunity—if the men were all working together, they would keep together. The rule down below was the vote. According to Urzúa, with thirty-three men, any issue would have a majority, and everyone would have had his say. That may not have been true at first, if there were really three different clusters of men. But still, voting worked to bring the men together. "You just have to speak the truth and believe in democracy." That was how he was going to save his men: by telling them what they really faced, and by making sure everyone shared and believed in their common decisions.

There were twenty cans of tuna fish, one can of peaches, one can of salmon, and some crackers in the shelter. Since there was no way to know how long the fish would have to last, the ration was tiny. "We talked about it at the first meeting we had when we were trapped," Villarroel recalled. "We all agreed that we should all share the food that was there. You just had to rough it. Every twenty-four hours eat a small piece of tuna. Nothing else."

"Small" meant as little as possible, about half a soda-bottle-cap-full, every twelve hours, along with a sip of milk, which was turning sour, a bite of canned peach, and a cracker. Oily water, drained from the large containers set aside to be used for machines, which the men found stashed throughout the mine shafts, joined the milk. They all knew how much food there was. They had voted on how to use it. And then Urzúa suggested they all eat together, in the same place, at the same time.

As long as the food lasted, it would belong to all of them. There was no chance to cheat, no possibility that someone else was getting extra on the side. It was hard, but equally hard for everyone. In those very first decisions, Sepúlveda and Urzúa took leadership—as a voice of the group. The bond holding them together was stronger than any one man.

Water. The men had machines that could claw down into the earth, and there is water below the desert. But every time you run an engine in a closed space, you feed car exhaust into the air you breathe. They needed to create a well with as little use of the machinery as possible.

Urzúa set them on the well-digging task, then sent another crew to map out the space around them. They needed to dig another smaller hole—their bathroom. Of course they needed water and a place for their waste, but all this action served another purpose—it changed hope from thirty-three frail and separate dreams into a shared goal they were working toward together. You only need water if you will survive. In each of their minds they were scared. But as a group they were acting like people who will be rescued, who are preparing for their rescue, who are building their own path to safety.

In those first days, there were fights in the mine and there was strength in the mine. No one could know which would crack first: the men's tempers or their hope.

CHAPTER FIVE

AUGUST 8–10: HOPE

AUGUST 8–9 **ABOVE** CAMP

Hope. That was the impossible, nearly invisible thread linking Urzúa's men trapped below and their anxious families above. "I know it may sound hard to believe," said Pedro Contreras, the uncle of one of the miners, "but we can't lose hope."

By the time the sun had burned off the night cold, some three hundred people had collected at the mine site—a mix of family, friends, fellow miners, engineers, experts, and government ministers. José Vega, the seventy-year-old miner who had warned his son Richard not to keep working at San José, dashed to the mine as soon as he heard of the collapse. "I'm not the kind of person to sit there with my arms crossed and crying," he told a reporter. "My son needs my help and I'm going after him." Vega was there to help and not just to wait. He'd brought another son and four others—if no one else could save the men down below, he was going to hack at the rocks himself.

The restless miners and their families were determined to stay until their relatives came back—alive or dead. A bonfire was fine for one night, but not for a vigil that could last a week or more. A tent city started to grow near the mine. But hope was like a dancing wind—one moment the campsite brought people together, helping one another, the next someone started sobbing, another yelling, and the hillside was a cauldron of angry emotions about to boil over.

Minister Golborne needed to keep one eye on the rescue efforts and another on the needs and moods of the community, which

Reporters rushed to the San José Mine when word came of its collapse and the trapped men. But at first their stories were mainly about frustration, anger, and disappointment.

now also included a growing set of news reporters serving as the eyes and ears of the watching world. He had nothing good to tell the press: "We have gone from hours to days and now possibly a rescue that could take weeks," he announced on Monday, the ninth. Then, speaking for himself, but also clearly for the relatives, he added that it is "very painful for us and generates a feeling of anger and powerlessness." The media now had two stories to cover: the rescue effort and the rising tide of blame. Who was at fault? Why had men been sent into an unsafe mine? Why were there no escape routes? Who let his happen?

AUGUST 10 **ABOVE** PRAYER

Saint Lawrence is the patron saint of mining in Chile, and this was his day. The Chileans called the entire effort to save the men *Operación San Lorenzo*—the Saint Lawrence mission. Faith can be seen as a stronger version of hope. It is hope plus—hope and belief, hope and trust. The Catholic bishop, Caspar Quintana, held a mass on the site on the saint's day. The statue of the Virgin of Candelaria—the focus of the shrine and two celebrations in Copiapó—was brought to San José. Bishop Quintana promised it would remain there as long as the rescue continued. Soon the hillside would be filled with shrines, statues, and posters of religious figures. Later thirty-three flags—thirty-two of Chile, one of Bolivia (for Carlos Mamani, the one foreign miner)—would flap bravely in the wind nearby. It was as if the deep feelings of the relatives needed to come out, to be visible; they could not stay inside. The statues and flags were like electrical towers—a way for people to beam their yearnings down into the black earth and up into the silent sky.

Most people in Chile are Catholic and the presence of the bishop and the statues must have fed their hope and their faith. But the bishop was not the only religious leader on the site. Carlos Parra Diaz, a Seventh-day Adventist pastor, soon arrived, offering counsel and prayer. He was later joined by Marcelo Leiva, a Baptist pastor, and Javier Soto, an evangelical minister. Whatever rivalry there may have been between the religious groups, they were serving the same end—offering comfort when no one else seemed to have any to offer.

For a while the men and machines trying to dig down to the miners were feeling optimistic. They estimated they were about 900 feet away but heading in the right direction—good progress. But they soon realized they were not actually following the path down that they had mapped out. At best they were about forty feet off from where they wanted to be. Their calculations might have been off, but the layout of the mine also kept changing. "The situation is very complex," President Piñera said. "The mine continues to have collapses."

Nothing the engineers had tried was working or was likely to work. "This is not easy . . . ," the president admitted. "The situation is now not only in our hands, but also in the hands of God. . . ."

Was there no hope? The families in the camp—the miner's wives, children, nieces, nephews, grandchildren, and friends—were now all the more alone. Their husbands, fathers, uncles, grandfathers, heroes—for one of the trapped miners was Franklin Lobos, a one-time soccer star and local favorite—were being left entombed.

ABOVE DRILL

Fidel Baez is an extremely experienced manager at CODELCO. While emotions rose and fell at the mine, Baez was slowly and carefully reading, thinking, and planning. For it was his job to sort through all of the offers of help that had been coming to Chile and to select the best possible strategy for saving the men. Baez was certain the miners were alive and could be rescued. The question was *how*.

If there was no way to reopen the mine and go down, what else could they do? As Baez laid out all of the e-mails that had come in, he saw the answers—nine of them. There were at least nine drills that could be brought to San José. The drills could go down through the earth, even if the ground kept shifting. It would be like ice fishing, but instead of aiming through ice for fish, they were going down through layers of stone to find life. They would keep drilling down until they got through the solid rock, and reached the shelter. If the miners were alive, that is where they had to be.

Kelvin Brown is an expert at guiding the very sophisticated drills made by Reflex Instruments, where he is an executive. The only problem was, the company, Brown, and the equipment were in Australia. On August 15 a military airplane dropped Brown and his drill off at Copiapó.

This first shot shows the interior of the C-130 cargo plane that brought Kelvin Brown, his drill, and his team to Chile. Upon landing, the men and their equipment were quickly unloaded and rushed to the mine site.

BELOW WHAT DO YOU SEE UNDERGROUND?

"When you turn off the lights in an underground mine," Dr. Chavez explains, "if you open your eyes wide and stare, you seem to see wavy lines, like heat in the darkness." Ron Mishkin agrees, "in the pitch black you see colored lights." There you are, in thick blackness, seeing strange sights. And then something goes wrong— you slip where you shouldn't have slipped, or a rock falls where you were sure there were no loose rocks. You know you are far away from the land of kids and trees and homes and friendly faces. It is very easy to believe you are in someone else's kingdom, the land of a spirit you need to win over or pay off or distract.

There are many legends about the nasty creatures that live in the depths of mines. In Germany, mischievous mine spirits were called *kobolds*. The element cobalt, as in cobalt blue, owes its name to the mythical creatures because it gives off noxious fumes when burned, as if a sprite were punishing you for touching it. In Cornwall, England, one of the oldest areas of tin mining in the world, it was believed that little, hideous demons lived in the tin and copper mines and hated miners. If miners heard knocking on the rock walls they knew they had better start running, because a cave-in was about to start. To this day, these demons are known as Tommyknockers. There are similar legends throughout South America. The miners in Potosí kiss a devil figure as they descend into the earth. Miners in Peru respect a gnomelike figure. And Dr. Chavez heard a tale in Chile of a female spirit that insisted that no women or priests enter the mine.

Hell is often pictured as a place of fire deep within the earth, and that association of earth, evil, and another realm inhabited by weird creatures exists in many parts of the world. Perhaps we always feel we are stealing from the earth when we descend down into it to find its treasures. If we are like thieves, we must be entering the realm of dark creatures. Or maybe it is because light and air are so important to us—they speak of spring, summer, and growth. So to go down, away from the sun, into the earth, is to enter another kingdom. But underground is not always linked with sprites, gnomes, and devils. It can also be a place where a person's spirit is tested.

The ancient Egyptians believed that after death a person's fate was decided in a ceremony held deep underground, in the kingdom of the god Osiris. The dead heart was weighed against truth, which was as light as a feather.

Greek myths tell of Hercules and Orpheus entering Hades. Some scholars believe those stories are the outlines of actual rituals, where Greeks entered caves and had to pass tests in order to be initiated into special cults.

For the ancient Greeks, going down into the darkness of a cave gave you the chance to look inside yourself. The very darkness removed distractions and allowed you to look fearlessly into an

This cave at Eleusis, near Athens, was the site of annual celebrations of the goddess Demeter. Caves such as this were used for special, secret ceremonies.

inner mirror. So rather than being the home of alien, evil beings, the cave was the testing place where you could examine yourself—like a Native American on a vision quest.

In those first moments of swirling dust Franklin Lobos, the former soccer star turned miner, could have been separated from the other men. But he thought he saw something like a "white butterfly" leading him back to the shelter. He was not a religious man, but he began to believe. In the silence and dark, other men were looking at their lives—at bad choices they had made, people they had hurt. It was as if they were all Jonah, swallowed up inside a whale, and wondering why—what have I done? What could I do better from now on? Mario Gómez, the oldest of the trapped men, took a place alongside Sepúlveda and Urzúa. Sepúlveda was the energetic cheerleader, Urzúa was their captain, their planner, the man who guided their actions. But Gómez now became their priest, their healer who could nurse their faith.

Drilling gave the rescue workers above ground a new focus, but it felt very different down in the mine—the rescue effort was the most agonizing tease. Lobos would hear the grinding up above, shaking the rocks below. "When the noise sounded close, his spirits rose. He felt alive. But each time, the drill pulled away, the noise fading to silence." He began to pray as he had never done before. But there was something else down in the mine that linked him back to his old life. Urzúa had been a soccer coach, and the men in the mine were becoming a kind of team. "The really great teams," Lobos said later, "are the really bonded ones. I didn't know many of the people I was working with when we were trapped, but when it happened, we pulled together." The tiny bit of food they shared held them together.

Urzúa was a map maker, and he was planning. He divided the men into groups, each with its own task. The trucks down in the mines could not drive the men out, but Urzúa knew they could be useful in other ways, so one group of men was assigned to keep them in running order. Edison Peña rigged together enough lamps and generators and truck engines to fend off the dark and provide a glow of light. Another group carefully watched over and divided up the food. Gómez was the spiritual leader, and Yonni Barrios, who had had a bit of medical training years earlier, was the doctor. Everyone was occupied. They had a goal, a purpose.

No one was permitted to go off alone for very long. "We worked hard for our own rescue," Urzúa explained. Every light Pena turned on and every chore that each team completed tied them together, and gave them hope.

CHAPTER SIX

AUGUST 10–21: DRILLING BLIND

ABOVE THE NINE SENTINELS

Nine drills formed an arc at the mine—nine lifelines reaching down into the earth. Perhaps to some of the families those products of machine shops and science seemed like guardians, or like their own prayers given shape. Kelvin Brown, the Australian drilling expert, knew he was on a special mission. He usually guided a bit down to look for jewels or precious metal. Now he was after "human gold." That only made it more difficult to face each day.

Where there should have been planning, there was only frustration and chaos. "Everyone was trying very hard and very fast," recalled Brown, "but it was a little bit hopeless in the early days. It was just a real lot of people, too many people." The control room was bursting with some twenty-five workers yelling instructions, suggesting plans in English and Spanish—all desperate to help, but only adding to the confusion. "We all wanted to save the miners," Brown explains. But that desire also had a tinge of competition. The local drillers "wanted to be the first to hit the target" and that yearning was getting in the way. Their drills could go much more quickly than the one Brown brought, but they were "very inaccurate."

The first ten holes aimed straight at where the shelter was supposed to be—as if the machines could burrow through earth in a line as direct as the hopes and prayers of the families. Brown knew that would not work. By the time he arrived there were some fifteen holes in the ground and they were all "well off target." One drill stopped working hundreds of feet above where

With all good intentions, drills soon spread across the hillside.

the miners might be. Then another hit a gap, a cavern where there shouldn't have been one. Alejandro Olave is an expert at figuring out where a drill is going underground and when it is shifting away from the proper path. He knew why they were having so much trouble: The maps they were using "had not been updated." Brown was told that that the shelter might be anywhere within eighteen feet of where they were aiming. But the target itself was only about seven and a half feet wide. They were digging blind through thousands of feet of rock to find a small target, which was not where it was supposed to be. That is way too much room for error.

Not only had the mine owners neglected to provide escape routes, but they did not even have accurate diagrams of their own diggings. You can calculate how to dig your way to a small space deep under the earth. But you cannot see it. They could drill to the center of the Earth and never reach the men, who might be sealed off, inches away from the hole.

Olave was worried, as was Brown. Brown estimated that it would take ten days to correct the existing holes and get onto the right path again, which was surely too long for the trapped men. The one chance was to start a new and better hole. The Chileans agreed. But there was a problem. Brown's arrival had been made very public to the waiting families. He was the expert, the hero who would save their relatives. Everyone was watching him—he had to be seen at the mine bustling around using the equipment. If he stopped drilling, the families would despair. So he had to make a show of work that was not going to succeed, even as they planned a better path down through the rock.

Brown's double role made it harder at the end of each day as he walked by the families. The camp had grown. Parents brought their young children. Slowly the space was being organized—a school here, a play area there, plenty of wood to keep fires burning, free dinners and crates of fruit, ever more statues of saints. But none of the gifts mattered. The only thing anyone wanted was hope, which Brown could not offer. "I wasn't prepared for it," Brown said, "the sheer number of people and the mood, you could feel it as well as see it in the children, the adults, brothers and sisters. It was very sad, somber, a lot of people looking down at the ground, looking into you, and that happened every day."

In April of 2006 a mine collapsed in Australia. One man was killed immediately but most of the miners made it out as the rocks were falling. That left Brant Webb and Todd Russell trapped below. After five days rescuers made contact with them, and were soon able to send in small supplies. Two weeks after the two miners were swallowed by the earth, they were saved. Two weeks—that was about as long as the thirty-three men might have to survive. Or maybe less—ten days since no one knew if they had supplies. Every failed hole, every mistake in the maps shortened that timeline.

Misleading maps made it very difficult to locate the shelter—the one place where the men might still be alive. But the drilling went on around the clock.

"After several days," Brown told a reporter, "it did start to weigh on me quite heavily and I thought *you know the best I can offer these people is death*." He did not think he could save the miners. "I just honestly gave them no chance." The only tiny bit of hope he had was that one of the last miners who had escaped reported that there was more air down below than the rescuers first thought. So maybe, possibly, someone was alive.

BELOW, THE ONE WORD NO ONE COULD SPEAK

Urzúa kept order. Every day there was a meeting. By the end of the first week, the food ration was reduced. At first they had enjoyed the luxury of a bite of tuna every twelve hours, but that was quickly changed to once every twenty-four. By the ninth day the single capful came every thirty-six hours. Gómez led them in prayer. But they were suffering. They were hot, dirty, sick, starving, and hearing the drillings above them gnawing at the rock only confirmed how desperate their situation was, since no one seemed to know where to find them. The sound fed Richard Villarroel's sense of despair, "the probes were so far away so we had no hope." Some of the other miners were sinking. Their eyes were still tearing from the dust that had blown into them during the collapse. Others had red rashes on their bodies, or needed daily medicines they had no hope of getting. Those addicted to cigarettes yearned for what they could not have. "This hell is killing me," Segovia later wrote. "I try to be strong, but I dream we are in an oven and when I wake I find myself in this eternal darkness." Mario Sepúlveda, the man whose energy and passion kept up everyone's spirits, wrote a farewell letter to his thirteen-year-old son: "Take care of your mother, your sister," he urged, for "you are now the man of the house."

Trapped inside of a mine, nothing changes. There are no clouds, no sky. There is just the same black, solid immovable rock. The thirty-three men were imprisoned in a cell no one could unlock.

Urzúa had promised to be realistic, and he was. Every day, Villarroel recalled, the captain "told us to have strength. If they find us they find us, if not, that's that." The tiny rations were taking their toll. The men needed to work, to do chores, to take care of their space. But working while hardly eating means only one thing: Your body begins to consume itself. Villarroel felt in himself and saw in the shriveling bodies of his fellow miners that "we started to eat ourselves up and get skinnier and skinnier." Their leader was insisting that they face this decline together—wherever it led. They all agreed because there was one story no one dared to mention.

In 1972 an airplane carrying forty-five people, including a professional rugby team from Uruguay, crashed in the Andes on its way to Chile. Seventy-two days later two members of the team made it to civilization, bringing word that fourteen more passengers were still alive. This was the most impossible story of survival under terrible conditions. But no one in the mine would breathe a word of it. That is because, lost in the snow and ice of the mountains, the passengers realized there was one, and only one, way that anyone might make it home: The living would eat the frozen flesh of the dead. It was almost impossible to make themselves do it—*almost* impossible. But not doing that would have meant certain death for everyone.

Cannibalism is the nightmare choice that arises in people's minds whenever they are cut off from food. People without food have been known to eat the bark off wooden posts. They have chewed on leather belts and shoes. They have quieted their bellies with grass, dirt, mud—anything to stop their bodies from demanding food, anything to put off that moment when they must make the terrible decision about human flesh. Urzúa was determined that it would never come up. They would live together or starve together.

CHAPTER SEVEN

AUGUST 21–22: HUMAN GOLD

AUGUST 21 **BELOW**

The men were living on about two hundred calories a day; they had each lost nearly fifteen pounds. At least half of them had no fat anymore, which meant their bodies were consuming their own muscles. The rations were always the same so it was easy to see how much food they had to eat: two days' worth. Seeing how little they had left, the men now limited themselves to one bite every three days. They could last two more days in the routine of chores, prayer, and food. And then what? Yonni Barrios, who was acting as the team doctor, knew the end was near. "We were all waiting to die."

Still, for the moment, Urzúa was holding them together, and no one would speak the forbidden word: cannibalism.

AUGUST 21 **ABOVE**

The families had had enough of watching, hoping, and worrying. They were mad at the company that had put their men in danger, at a government that had looked the other way, at all the swirling experts from around the world who drilled and drilled and drilled and got nowhere. They were tired of waiting, tired of being frightened, tired of not knowing anything. "It was getting extremely tense," Brown recalls. Men were pushing at the police, insisting that they be given their own chance to go in, to find their relatives. The mood was like "a powder keg," and something big, bad, and violent was going to happen very soon.

Down below, the miners saw the end coming, felt hope slip away. Two thousand feet above them, their families felt it too—the time for patience was over, the waiting could not go on. As we can see it now, they were on opposite ends of an emotional bridge—out of touch with one another, but somehow on two sides of exactly the same feeling.

There was no more time.

Brown had a very good drill and a very big problem. The drill bit was studded with diamond chips—it could slide through rock, it was guided by magnets, and eased along by high-pressure water. But he had to dig down through two kinds of materials: slabs of thick, hard rock—mostly feldspar—and then layers of "softer material." That combination makes it especially hard to stick to one line. The drill stays true as it bites through the rock, then shifts as its slides through softer areas. The drilling team has to keep surveying and adjusting to stay on course. But no matter how often they had to make corrections, the drilling could not stop.

AUGUST 22, 2:00 AM **ABOVE**
Brown was woken up and brought to the site. The drill was about 450 feet above where the shelter should be and they needed him to make one last measurement and correction.

3:00 AM **ABOVE**
The Schramm T685 drill was eating down when it suddenly hit a large airspace. The driller turned off the machine and slowly lowered it down.

BELOW
First they must have heard it, chewing down closer and closer. Then a round, knobby, metal circle looking like a large shower

head crashed through the ceiling of the shelter. Someone was smart enough to begin hitting the drill.

ABOVE

Tapping—the driller felt the vibration. Their drill was off, but something—no, someone—was touching it, hitting it, sending a message. The crew called a paramedic to put a stethoscope on the drill. There it was, a pulse in the mine, as in a body—life. Someone was alive, right there, where the drill went.

BELOW

Urzúa rushed to find paint, and the men covered the drill with red. Mario Gómez wrote a letter to his wife and José Ojeda scrawled a message to the world. The pieces of paper were put in a bag and taped to the drill—as safely and carefully as only miners know how.

ABOVE

The tapping stopped, the drill pulled up, up, up, until it emerged from the mine—blazing red and holding two pieces of paper:

Estamos bien en el refugio los 33
"We are in the shelter and are well, the 33"

Alive, safe, in a known place, and all together.
The camp exploded . . . with joy.

The actual note that José Ojeda sent from the depths of the mine.

AROUND THE WORLD
AND INTO SPACE

CHAPTER EIGHT

CAMP HOPE

YOU HAVE NEVER SEEN such leaping, shouting, hugging and hugging and hugging whoever was standing there. Picture New Year's, Mardi Gras, a last-second Super Bowl touchdown, and a seventh game of the World Series walk-off home run, all rolled into one. The tears everyone was holding back flipped upside down and came out as happy screams, wild leaps, crazy dances. Some genius gave the gathering place of the relatives the perfect name: *Campamento Esperanza*, "Camp Hope." First Copiapó, then Chile's capital city of Santiago, had instant sound tracks as drivers paraded through the streets honking their horns.

The news media rushed back—reporters and camera crews sent word of the spectacular note and the wonderful news everywhere from China, Israel, and India to Australia and England, to Canada, Jordan, and Nepal, to Guyana, and all across South America and the United States. The mine that no one cared about was now the center of the world's attention.

President Piñera flew back to the mine, so he could hold the note high in the air and beam.

Contact—the rescuers had reached the men. That was wonderful. It changed everything. A temporary phone hookup snaked down the Schramm hole let Urzúa speak directly to the president: What do you need? Piñera asked. "Don't abandon us," came the reply. "You won't be left alone. Nor have you been alone for a single moment," Piñera assured him, his men, and the nation.

Now the men could tell the world what they needed—food, medicine, clothes, word from their families—and all of those relief

The press drifted away in days when there was little to report. As soon the miners' note arrived, every form of media arrived to tell the thrilling story.

supplies could snake their way down to the shelter. The miners had made it this far in the dark, alone. Now, for sure, they would be cared for and would survive . . . longer. But that is all contact meant. The hole was only about five and a half inches around—a grapefruit might squeeze through it, but not a human being. Contact brought joy—and a new set of problems.

What was the best way to bring thirty-three starving, weakened men up, out from under two thousand feet of rock? How long would it take to make that possible? If that was days or weeks, fine. But what if it took months? The men had shown astonishing spirit and will, but could they keep that up for as long as the drillers might need? How could the rescuers know what the men needed to keep their minds clear and their hearts strong?

These were difficult challenges, but the note was not just a link between the men down below and the drillers on the surface. It was also a flag waved to the entire world—*here we are, we did our part, we saved ourselves, now you find a way to bring us home*. And, all over the world, experts on everything the miners could possibly need listened and rushed to respond.

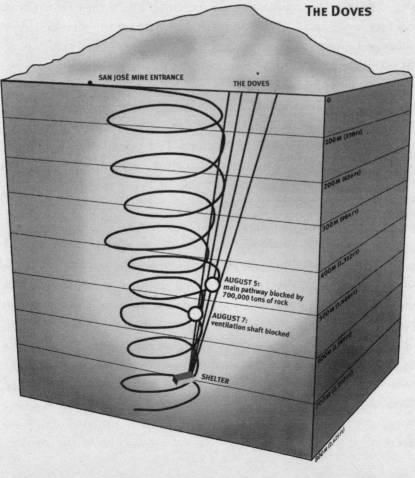

THE DOVES

SAN JOSÉ MINE ENTRANCE

THE DOVES

0

100 M (328 FT)

200 M (656 FT)

300 M (984 FT)

400 M (1,312 FT)

AUGUST 5:
main pathway blocked by
700,000 tons of rock

500 M (1,640 FT)

AUGUST 7:
ventilation shaft blocked

600 M (1,969 FT)

700 M (2,297 FT)

SHELTER

800 M (2,625 FT)

PALOMA

Paloma means dove, the symbol of peace. But it can also mean something more like carrier pigeon—the bird that brings messages. First one, then two, and finally three steel-lined holes were drilled down to the shelter. Then a relay system was cobbled together that turned those small tunnels into tiny elevators, which were soon named *paloma*s, the little birds of hope, the carrier pigeons of the mines. The *paloma*s were white tubes that could fit into the approximately five-inch holes, they were about six feet long, and capped on both ends. Anything that could be squeezed, bent, crushed, or taped so that it was small enough to fit into that space could be sent down to the miners, or up from them to the topside world.

Every run of the *paloma* express lasted thirty minutes, and they kept going around the clock. It took about ten minutes for gravity to pull a *paloma* down the 2,100 feet. The miners were given ten minutes to unload it. And then a winch spent another ten minutes hauling it up. The little birds brought down food, medicines, toothpaste, inhalers for those having trouble breathing, clothing, playing cards and dominos, books and magazines, tiny bibles, a crucifix, a picture of a pretty girl, paper to write on, and toilet paper to use. A Richmond, Virginia, company mailed a load of special socks that helped keep the miners' feet free of infections. A video camera flew down, a film showing the world the men had built for themselves shot back up. That was before people started to get creative. The miners were sleeping on rock and mud. Someone figured out that a cot could be fitted into the tubes—so soon the miners had beds. A charged iPod filled with music went down, then came up every few days to get more juice. The Japanese company Sony sent PlayStations preloaded with games—for men who were tired of cards and dominos.

These lifeless hills framed the San José Mine. Only the hope of finding ore underground could bring people to such a grim spot.

The colored tents show the growing area set aside for families waiting for word of the men trapped beneath the San José Mine.

The crew who reached the miners, working at their drill on the day they made contact.

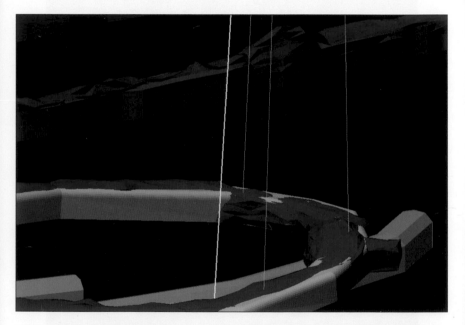

Drillers could not see into the earth. But by using existing mine maps and constantly updated data, they could generate computer models of their work. This image shows Kelvin Brown's drill—the thin green line on the right—hitting the area of the shelter, the red area on the right curve of the mine. The blue, and farther up, purple areas are images of the pathway of the mine. This computer image is a close-up of the shelter area. To view a computer image of a larger section of the mine, see insert, page 6.

OPPOSITE, TOP: Thirty-two Chilean flags and one for Bolivia decorated the hillside, a salute from above to the men below.

OPPOSITE, BOTTOM: The sentinels, hard at work.

This computer image shows the existing bore hole line Brandon Fisher needed to expand. The twisting red, orange, and then blue shape is the pathway of the mine; the straight yellow line is the existing shaft. The loop near the top where the yellow line almost touches the red is the 262-meter level where the Center Rock drill hit the roof bolt. The tight blue section near the bottom was at the 520-meter level, but the drillers got through it with no difficulty. Fisher and his team did not know how close they were going to come to the existing mine shafts until after they started drilling.

As the *paloma*s sped up and down they carried enough equipment to set up video links with the trapped men. This screen capture was taken on August 29.

The captain is free: Luis Urzúa emerges from the Phoenix. All of the men are safe—mission accomplished.

NASA scientists took these two pictures showing the *paloma* team at work. The long thin cylinders were carefully stuffed full of needed goods and personal messages, then sent up and down the thin shafts that connected the miners and the outside world.

NASA, which runs the American space program, says there are five stages in a crisis: the incident that sets it off, making sure people survive, sustaining them once help is on the way, rescuing them, then helping them, and their families, recover. The miners handled the first two beautifully—they escaped the disaster and kept themselves alive. In fact, they did everything NASA teaches its own astronauts to do. They found their leaders, split up their chores, and kept themselves occupied with work that really mattered. But those two steps were only the start. The next challenge was the slow recovery, and the race to drill holes large enough to bring them out.

Chile has a long border with the Pacific, and thus a navy complete with submarines. The Minister of Health quickly realized that, if anyone could understand what the trapped men needed it would be a submarine commander, so he contacted Captain Renato Navarro Genta. Captain Navarro (in Spanish-speaking countries a last name is often the mother's maiden name and is not always used) was the head of Chile's submarine schools, and a former sub commander. He knew what it was like to live in a confined space, but also how to plan for emergencies when the closest help may be thousands of feet overhead. Navarro was now responsible for "the life support of every miner." He had to figure out what state they were in, what they needed, and how to get them out.

Captain Navarro and his team began to sketch out a kind of Earth-traveling, one-man subterra—a capsule that could safely shoot a man up from underground. But designing and building that escape route would take time, and depended entirely on carving out much larger holes than now went down to the shelter. There would be time to plan the capsule, so long as the men were healthy enough to wait. Navarro's first problem was to get medical information about the men.

Yonni Barrios had a new role. It was his job to gather blood samples so doctors could find out the exact condition of each miner. The men were starving, but the worst thing you can do is hand someone who is wasting away platefuls of food. There is a good chance that will kill him. If a person does not have enough key vitamins and minerals, such as phosphate, potassium, or niacin, eating can trigger a heart attack. Barrios filled thirty-three test tubes with blood and sent them up. Then down came vitamins and vaccines—the hot, humid mine was a perfect home for germs and viruses, and the last thing the men needed was to start spreading pneumonia or flu. Barrios made sure the men brushed their teeth, and was sent a short how-to video on dentistry, along with sterilized tools in case he had to pull an infected tooth.

Tested, measured, slowly and carefully fed, their rashes salved with creams, the dust in their eyes being washed away, the daily medicines they had missed now flying down on schedule and on time, the men were being sustained. They were not getting worse and slowly, one by one, at their own pace, their bodies were starting to heal. That left their hearts and minds.

LOVE LETTERS

The yellow, white, and orange-red tent city now bulged with some 1,100 parents, grandparents, uncles, aunts, cousins, children, wives, and girlfriends. While Captain Navarro was figuring out how to help the miners recover their physical health, Kristian Jahn was mobilizing a team of twenty-three psychologists to support their families. The relatives could finally begin to push their fears away, opening a floodgate of other feelings.

The threat of losing Mario made Lilianett Gómez realize how deeply she loved him. "Can you imagine?" she asked. "After thirty years of marriage we will start sending each other love letters again.

I want to tell him that I love him so much. I want to tell him that things will be different, that we will have a new life." Lilianett suddenly became a young bride planning. Their marriage had been a simple vow in an office, they'd never had a church wedding. When Mario came back, they would go before the altar together and the bells would ring. She set out to pick the perfect dress.

Once the miners' basic needs were met, they were showered with love and presents. Leonardo Farkas, a Chilean businessman, arrived bringing ten-thousand-dollar cheques for the families of every one of the trapped men. The Chilean national soccer team all signed a shirt and sent it down to Franklin Lobos and that only began the T-shirt brigade. The top soccer team Real Madrid sent thirty-three signed shirts, and then a new bright green shirt with the words "Fuerza Mineros," which could be read as "Be Strong, Miners," was printed up and sent down. Tapes of South America's greatest soccer heroes, Argentina's Diego Maradona and Brazil's Pelé, followed—to inspire the men. Edison Peña's family got him a photo of his own hero, the American rock-'n'-roll pioneer, Elvis Presley.

The mines beamed back the same strong feelings—and more. Mario Gómez told Lilianett that "I haven't stopped thinking about all of you for a single moment." One miner wrote to Cristina, his girlfriend, "Hello, my love, I hope you are not sad." Then he listed everything he was looking forward to eating when he arose from the earth: "pancakes, sweet fritters, roast chicken with French fries, grilled steak." The letter ended with a private note Cristina would not let anyone see. "We never wrote each other letters before," Cristina explained. "But now it's almost like we're dating again." Her aunts, though, were sure they knew what was on those last lines. The couple had been together for years, but she had never agreed to take the next step. Now she was the one who had suggested they get married.

The dry hills near the mine were increasingly covered with messages, images, prayers, and gifts for the miners.

Separated by two thousand feet of rock, couples, siblings, parents, and children were vowing to grow closer than they had ever been before. "This was more than a miracle," said the father of one of the miners at his tent in Camp Hope. "It's like being reborn again."

A new life was not as clear a path for some of the miners who had been in troubled relationships when they left for work on August 5. Many of the men who worked at San José had led tough, hard lives—they did not have model families with a waiting wife, two sweet kids, and picture-postcard emotions. Camp Hope was now a small town where the sound of gossip and juicy scandal began to be heard. With so many reporters stationed near the camp, every family drama instantly became news everywhere around the world—except down in the mine. Officials controlled the letters, to make sure nothing reached the men that might disturb them. Still, the miners knew well enough if there were bruised feelings and tangled romances waiting for them topside. Indeed as they prayed down inside the mine, many resolved to return as more attentive fathers, more caring husbands, better men.

The officials at the mine watched over the letters, and soon phone calls and videos that went up and down through the earth. But family messages were the least of their worries. They were starting to realize that they had some very bad news to give the men.

RESCUE PLANS

PLAN A: "THE TURTLE"

A Strata 950 drill lumbered south to start the actual rescue, which sounded good—at first. The only way to smash enough rock to carve out an escape shaft for the miners was to find the best drills and drill teams from anywhere. These drills had to be huge—there could not be a repeat of the chaos of the nine sentinels. The Chileans had a great deal of knowledge and skill, but they were also smart enough to know when to ask for help. This was one of those moments, which is why the Canadian drill was on its way.

Some of the families kept insisting that there was a better way to free the men: just blast a hole through the rock that sealed them in. Off hand that could seem simplest and easiest. After all, once past the fallen rocks, there was a safe road up from the mine to the surface. But there was one terrible risk in that approach: The mine was unstable, and explosions large enough to clear a path to the men might just as well let loose new rock slides that would kill them. If the men were not going to be freed along the existing road, there were only two alternatives: get at them through another mine entrance or carve a new channel straight down to them. The last choice was by far the fastest and safest. But what was the best way to dig that new hole?

There are many different ways to drill through rock, each of which has its advantages and disadvantages depending on the specific terrain involved, so picking how to drill is often as important as deciding where to drill. The Chileans decided to use this fact to their advantage—they would create a kind of great race by giving three different types of drills a chance to save the men. If one team turned out not to be the best for the San José, another might be just right. The three tools the Chileans decided to try were a raise borer drill used mainly for mining, a cluster drill (also known as percussion hammer) used for carving out water wells, and a behemoth, used to look for oil. Let the best drill and drill team win! With one additional rule: You had to be able to get your drill to the site . . . fast.

Cementation, Inc., a mining company with arms in many parts of the world, happened to have a drill working at a mine not far from San José digging a ventilation shaft. They offered to send it to the mine, and so the Strata 950 arrived at the site. The massive rig was one of only five of its type in the world. It weighed forty tons and was extremely reliable . . . and painfully slow.

As Dr. Chavez explains, "Raise borers do just that—they drill holes large enough for 'raises,' which are essentially large-diameter (up to perhaps three feet or so) tubes." Mines need shafts—either for rocks to tumble down or for air to flow in and out. A raise is simply a tube that lines a mine shaft. "Raise-bore" then means to make or bore a hole to allow space for a raise. This kind of drill work requires two steps. First you drill a pilot hole, a smaller channel that runs to your endpoint in the mine. Once you have reached your goal, you change drill bits. Now a very large bit travels back up from the bottom, carving out a large, clean hole.

A drill is only as good as the team that runs it. That's why a phone began ringing in an underground mine in Timmons, Ontario. Gene Fallon, a driller who knew how to manage the Strata, picked up. "Get . . . back to North Bay," his supervisor said. "You're flying to Chile tomorrow." Fallon reached San José and found a team of South Africans and Chileans that Cementation, Inc. had managed to shift from other work there to help him.

Dr. Michael Duncan, head of the NASA team, standing next to the Strata—the Turtle.

The Strata was a good choice because it was able to drill down on a dead-straight line, gauging out just enough room to fit a chute that could carry the men to safety. Since the shelter had been located and mapped, it was not hard to figure out where to place the rig: a direct shot some two thousand feet above the refuge. The Strata looks a bit like a version of R2-D2 from *Star Wars* when the robot has its arms extended—shiny metal poles anchor a large central drum. First, three bits from that drum drilled a thin hole about fifteen inches across, much like the channel that carried the *paloma*s. Once that column reached all the way to the miners, the second bit was slated to open up the space—nearly doubling the column to twenty-eight inches across, wide enough to hold a man.

There was one obvious flaw with using the raise-bore method to save the miners in Chile: The entire system relied on drilling the larger hole up from the bottom. But the very problem at the San José Mine was that no one could get down to the miners. Back in Canada, the company's tool shop had to quickly figure out how to break that second drill into pieces that could go down to the miners, where they could reassemble and attach it.

Fallon spent his endless shifts watching a screen looking for any indication that the Strata had veered off course. Steady as she went, the drill held true. As he told Jennifer Yang of the *Toronto Star,* "We will hit the target. Guaranteed we will hit the target. We will." Yes, but when? Even though the machine worked twenty-four hours a day, one official admitted, "the disadvantage is the time. We call it the turtle plan." Based on the very slow progress of the Strata, officials believed it could take three or four months to get the men out of the mine. The miners were doing well—but how would they react to knowing they might well be trapped until Christmas?

HELP FROM OUTER SPACE

Chilean officials were not ready to give the bad news to the miners or the families yet. First they had to think about how to prepare them. On Monday, August 23, they made their first call to the organization that has gathered the most information about how human beings behave when they are isolated in hostile environments for long periods of time: NASA, the American space agency.

The best current guess is that a trip to Mars (the next planet we are likely to explore) will take at least six months, followed by a stay of up to a year and a half there until Earth and Mars again swing close enough to allow for a six-month-long flight back. Looking further ahead, in September of 2010, scientists announced that they had discovered Gliese 581 g, a "Goldilocks planet"—one that is not too hot and not too cold, so it just might be able to support life. If human beings had to leave Earth, perhaps we could relocate to Gliese 581 g, except that it is 120 trillion miles away. It would take so long to get there that we would have to set off into space knowing that, at best, our grandchildren might never leave the ship. Since NASA is responsible for making sure that anyone the American government sends into space handles it well, it has had to learn a lot about how people cope with being trapped.

NASA has studied people who go off to the Antarctic and are sealed in by the cold for months at a time. They have computers full of data on astronauts who have spun around the Earth, settled in on the Mir space station, and traveled to the moon and back. Scientists working for the space agency have isolated people in water tanks and kept tabs on the changing bodies of test subjects who lie in bed twenty-four hours a day for months at a time (no bathroom breaks, there are tubes for that). NASA (and the Russians who have similar interests in space flight) have counted precisely how much bacteria collects on your body when you haven't showered for a week, two weeks, three, and more—and exactly when you smell the worst to those around you. And NASA has paid particular attention to what happens to your mind in a spacecraft—what makes you able to work and play well with others while confined to a tin can, and what makes you annoyed, annoying, and even a potential danger. Anyone who follows the NFL draft knows how carefully pro-football teams study and test potential draftees, looking for any sign of an all-American who might fail as a professional. NASA does the same, only in even greater detail. They have much more to be concerned about than merely squandering a draft choice.

A mission to Mars carrying a vulnerable crew, costing billions, and watched anxiously by people on every continent cannot go awry because the astronauts don't get along. Dr. Norbert Kraft, who studies how people will behave on long space flights, explains the problem: "You're sleep-deprived . . . the bathroom stinks, and you have noise all the time. You can't open a window. You can't go home, you can't be with your family, you can't relax." Cooped up with your fellow flyers, you have soon heard every story they know, you can predict every thing they will say, you've memorized the punch line to every joke they want to tell. And yet, as astronaut Jim Lovell warns, "you're in a risky business and you depend on each other to stay alive. So you don't antagonize the other guy."

On August 25, the Chileans held a phone conference with their NASA counterparts, and soon a small group of doctors and psychologists was on its way to the mine. Dr. J. D. Polk, an air-evacuation expert, came to share his knowledge. Clint Cragg, an engineer on the team, happened to be a former submarine commander. As Captain Navarro explained, that immediately put him at ease. They spoke "'the same language,' and I am not talking about the English language." The two submariners quickly huddled together and exchanged ideas. Navarro's effort to create an escape capsule set off a million thoughts and plans in Cragg's mind. He "put together a team of engineers from almost every center around the agency" and within three days they sent a list of some fifty suggested design features and equipment choices.

Dr. Al Holland came as the psychologist on the NASA team and he had his eyes on the needs of three different groups: the miners and their families, of course, but also the helpers. In his work he has come to realize that, the success or failure of a mission is not just a result of individual strengths and weaknesses. As every sports coach says, you win as a team or you lose as a team. Everyone has some ability to shine, to rise to the occasion, in a crisis. Some, like Urzúa, will know how to lead. Others will understand that they best serve the cause by following. The most important thing is to make it possible for everyone to use their best abilities—to make sure no one felt so blocked or frustrated that he or she would undermine what everyone was desperate to do: save the men. Dr. Holland listened as Dr. Iturra, the lead Chilean psychologist, spoke to the miners, and began to picture what he might say to the families.

From Clint Cragg
10/11/10 and 10/14/10

Example suggested requirements:

1. EV [ESCAPE VESSEL] shall allow for a single
miner to enter and secure himself and the vehicle
for ascent. EV ingress shall also accommodate an
incapacitated miner, and should be operable by the
last person.
Rationale: Some miners may have injuries or medical
issues at the time of rescue. Eventually, only one
miner will be left in the mine shaft so there will
be no one to help him into the EV and prepare it
for ascent.

2. EV shall be self-aligning at both ends of the
escape shaft and during transit.
Rationale: The last miner to be extracted will
have no help in manually aligning the vehicle for
initial entry in the escape shaft. (for example,
potential EV self-alignment methods include rails,
funnels, etc).

3. EV shall be free to slide within the escape-
shaft. Any exterior surfaces shall be smooth with
no sharp edges or protrusions. Sufficient spare
parts or surfaces that contact the shaft walls
shall be provided to replace worn or broken parts.
Rationale: The escape shaft wall roughness may,
depending on design, cause significant wear during
operations.

This is an excerpt from the actual memo Clint Cragg and his team sent to Captain Navarro.

CHAPTER TEN

ABNORMAL–NORMAL

URZÚA HAD BEEN REALISTIC with his men from the start, and the authorities decided to do the same. The trapped miners were given the real timeline—with rescue a very long way off. Although there were some 250 mental health experts on hand to help the men, to everyone's relief the bad news did not upset them. Instead they took up the next challenge with the same spirit they had used to fend off fear and hunger. Now they would have to settle in to life underground.

The men understood that they were going to have to live as moles longer than any human beings ever had—for months on end—so they needed to turn their burrow into a kind of home. The NASA team had one initial suggestion for how to achieve that. Edison Peña's grid of generators and lamps had given his fellow miners some light, but the space experts had a new idea. The beams could be turned on and off in sixteen- and eight-hour shifts that would simulate day and night. The day was neatly divided into thirds—eight hours of sleep, eight hours of free time, eight hours of work—and there was plenty of work to do.

The doves rushing up and back brought enough food to have breakfast at 8:30, a snack two hours later, lunch at 1:00, and another bite at 5:30 before a full dinner at 9:00—a normal schedule for the men. In order to keep to the timetable, a three-man delivery team had to meet the doves as they landed, quickly off-load the next meal, and pass it along. After every meal another group cleaned up carefully, separating plastic from food like any good recycler, but also to keep their living space clean and as free of germs as possible.

After breakfast the men loaded up on a bulldozer to drive to an underground waterfall so they could shower—no one wanted to test NASA's careful calendar of when body odor reaches its peak, or dandruff begins to cascade from unwashed hair, like snow in winter.

Now that they had light and contact with the outside world, the men could spread out in the mine; they did not need to remain clustered near the shelter. And they needed to move. Any drill that cut through the earth toward them would, necessarily, send rock debris and water, which is used as part of the drilling process, flooding down the shaft. While the miners organized work crews to clear away the rock, the men needed to shift their eating and sleeping areas away from the mud and muck.

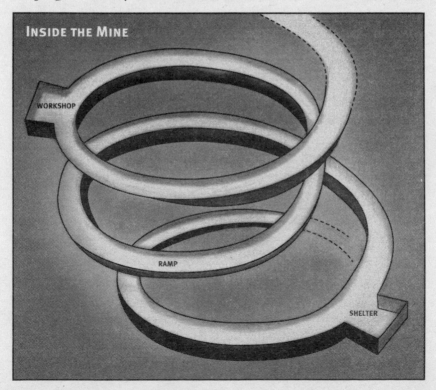

INSIDE THE MINE

WORKSHOP

RAMP

SHELTER

Urzúa used his mapping skills to figure out how the men could make best use of the mine—setting up one room for games and recreation, another as a chapel for prayer, and a small space, on the side and out of sight, for the newly established phone line. The miners would need privacy, so no one would see them crying when they spoke to their families.

Getting back to normal came in many ways.

Peña was a runner. By the time the miners made contact with the drillers, moving was the furthest thing from his mind. Weak, hungry, and waiting for death, he had curled up into a little ball, like a baby. But now that he was eating again and feeling better, he began training. He found a way to cut down his heavy boots so they just reached his ankles, and set out. "I ran to forget I was trapped," he later said. "I ran in the dark. . . . I went to the depths, the lowest of the low, but I kept running." Soon he was strong enough to cover some five miles a day. As Peña ran, he kept singing "Return to Sender," a song by his hero Elvis Presley. "I was saying to that mine, 'I can outrun you, I'm going to run until you're just tired and bored of me,' and I did it."

Dr. Mike Duncan, the leader of the NASA team, spoke with the miners by phone, his broken Spanish only lasting through "¿Cómo estás? . . . Bien," before a translator had to help out. Duncan was just one of many topside people who began sending encouragement down the mine. Thursday, September 2, brought bad and good news: the Strata 950 was moving so slowly it had gotten down to only about 130 feet, and worse, it would have to pause. Geologists had found a fault in the rock that made drilling dangerous. The rescue timeline now surely stretched out months ahead. But the doves carried a special gift—prayer beads and rosaries, blessed by the Pope and sent directly from Rome. For the miners, those who had been religious before the accident as well as those whose faith grew down in the mine, this was a powerful form of blessing.

On September 4, four people who had survived that terrible plane crash in the Andes in 1972 arrived. "Remain united and together," one urged the men. And then, looking ahead to life after their final rescue, the four offered some financial advice: Don't "give away too much." They knew from their own experience that there would soon be a scramble to publish books and film movies about the miracle of Chile. If everything continued to go well and the miners got home safely, the disaster that very nearly took their lives would be their ticket to fame and, very likely, fortune.

To round out the string of gifts, on September 8 the South Korean technology giant Samsung sent a new product, a cell phone that included a tiny projector preloaded with a message from President Piñero and, more important, the Chile–Ukraine soccer match. More than two thousand feet below ground, flickering on the rock wall, were the sights and sounds of the game so many of the miners wanted to see. In turn, a fiber-optic cable beamed images of Franklin Lobos and the other miners watching the game back out to the nation. "To Franklin Lobos, a special hello," said the game announcer, completing the loop of game, mine, and game.

AUGUST 25 ON TOPSIDE

The mood of weird normalcy down in the mine was matched up in the camp. Every evening at 6:00 family members gathered in a larger tent to hear reports on the progress of the drilling, the condition of the men, and the timeline stretching ahead. The NASA team arrived and was impressed at what they saw—the top leaders of the rescue, from government ministers to local officials, were all there to make sure the families had the most direct and current information. Looking at the packed tent of eighty or so seated women and standing men, Dr. Holland could see the concern on their faces. Yes, they were miners' families, but usually if there was an accident, a man either died or came back quickly. This long wait was different.

Bundled up against the nighttime cold, wearing clothes that hinted at hard lives, the families showed their needs. But Dr. Holland also felt something else—a bond linking everyone there. When a little child scampered up, anyone might take his or her hand— from the highest official to the closest grandmother. Together— they would get through this together. He had noticed that when Dr. Iturra spoke to the miners, the Chilean doctor expressed more feeling than was common—at least in his own Texan background. So when he spoke through an interpreter, he was eager to show he was not some outsider throwing his weight around, telling them what to do. He was there because their government had invited him, and he would offer what he could.

Dr. Holland gave the families a sense of what he saw in their faces. He could feel that they were having a hard time. To this day, when he speaks about that moment, his voice cracks. But, he explained, they were on a mission of their own, just like the miners. The families had as important a part to play in the rescue as anyone else. Their spirit, their encouragement, their support was a lifeline for the trapped men. He asked the families to have faith—not just a religious faith, but also a trust in the team that was working to rescue the men. And finally he urged them to realize that nothing was going to happen quickly. The rescue was going to be a marathon, not a sprint. And so he urged some of them to go home and to leave one family member on-site while letting others return to work or school, to their regular lives. The families liked that suggestion, and soon the camp shrank—until the weekends. Then, everyone flooded back—eager to share mail, calls, and videoconferences with the men.

Rolando González, in costume as Rolly the Clown, stayed at the camp throughout the crisis in order to entertain the youngest relatives of the trapped miners.

The little tent city had showers, kitchens, and scheduled concerts by visiting entertainers. For a while the press had been allowed to mingle with families, but now there were too many reporters. The rescue site was divided into rings: Camp Hope for the families; just two documentary makers, NOVA and Discovery; and the drilling area was only for specialists. That left an ever-growing circle for the media: reporters, photographers, TV crews (including five from Japan alone) and film directors getting the feel of the location. The British Broadcasting Corporation sent some twenty-five people to the site, and recruited Marcela, Ximena, and Omar, all grown children of Omar Reygadas, one of the trapped men, to keep diaries. Their entries traced the same events that we have just seen two thousand feet down.

On August 31, Marcela was worried about the muddy conditions in the mine, until she learned that the men were moving.

On September 1, Omar wrote that his dad was craving his "favorite food": steak with lots of avocado. But as the men got healthy enough to eat just about anything, the rescuers faced a new problem: The capsule was going to be tight, so the miners were going to have to watch their waistlines. Ironically, men who had been starving, wasting away, now had to be sure "to avoid getting fat."

On September 5, Omar met with the four famous survivors of the 1972 crash. They assured the families that "the miners will get out of there stronger than ever before."

Ximena reported that once a week, at exactly 2:30 in the afternoon, the moment of the initial rock collapse, everyone drove around honking their horns and blowing whistles—both marking the instant when the earth grabbed the men, and chasing it away, defeating it.

Two days later Ximena got to talk with her father by video-conference. "Our mission," she wrote, "is to give him lots of hope." Her father wanted pictures of his children and grandchildren but also had a more practical request: He needed plastic bags so that he could sort out his underwear and keep it dry.

Indeed, so many presents were rushing down to the men that the families needed to keep up. After all, united as they were in the mine, the men rooted for soccer teams that were archrivals. The guys who rooted for the University of Chile soccer team were bragging about their team, so Ximena sent down the flag of Colo-Colo, Omar's favorite squad.

CHAPTER ELEVEN

THE RACE DOWN

PLAN B: "THE RABBIT"

At 9:00 PM at night on Wednesday, July 24, 2002, a mine shaft 240 feet down at Quecreek in Somerset County, Pennsylvania, flooded. Nine men were trapped in the darkness, with cold water rushing in and very little air left to breathe. A Yost Drilling rig was rushed to the site to try to free them, but at 1:30 in the morning on Friday, it got stuck and broke. Center Rock, Inc., a small Pennsylvania drilling company, managed to fish out the broken pieces. A new drill reached the farm just above the mine. It sliced enough room through the rock to fit a rescue capsule, and by 2:45 AM on Sunday all nine men made it to safety. Tom Foy had been one of those men down in the coal mine and his family would not let him go back underground, so he took a job alongside Brandon Fisher, the founder of Center Rock, Inc.

Foy and Fisher heard the great news of August 22, when the miners' note came up attached to the end of Kelvin Brown's drill. But as they were leaving for church, Brandon and his wife, Julie, heard another radio report announcing that the men would remain trapped underground for months on end. They knew they could do better. "I don't know how we could have slept," Fisher told a reporter, "knowing we have a technology that could have helped."

"Well, heck," Foy recalls saying, "they ain't getting out till Christmastime, and I know and Brandon knows and we all knew we could get down to them faster than that." Fisher had helped save Foy's life. Now, with newer equipment, they were sure they could beat the existing timetable.

Fisher had two big problems. How could he convince the Chilean government to listen to his little firm? And if he did get their approval to drill, how could he ship twenty thousand pounds of equipment from Berlin, Pennsylvania, to the San José Mine? Like any student given a homework assignment, he and his partner Richard Soppe rushed to the Net. But of course there was no convenient article for them to consult. Instead they had to become a cross between a detective and a lawyer. First they needed to have a clear idea of the conditions at the mine site. What kind of rock was there? How deep was the mine? What layers and faults might he encounter? The Chileans would only listen to him if he showed that he had a detailed and accurate picture of their problem. Then he needed to prove that his equipment was reliable, tested, and suited for the challenge.

The Center Rock plan was completely different from the slow, steady lumbering of the Strata 950. Fisher intended to make use of the last of the three channels that was already ferrying the *paloma*s down to the shelter. First a twelve-inch drill would widen the existing five-inch space, then twenty-eight- and twenty-six-inch drills would follow, allowing just enough room for the escape capsule Captain Navarro and his team were building. This was a plan built for efficiency and speed—if it worked.

As soon as Fisher had his argument ready, he made use of the resources of his own state government. The Chilean government has very good connections with all of the best mining companies in the world. In turn, states such as Pennsylvania, which have a long mining history and strong mining companies, have representatives in Chile who stay in close touch with Chilean mining officials. Fisher reached his state representative who, in turn, put Center Rock's proposal in the right minister's hands.

By September 2, the ministers agreed that Center Rock should be given a chance to save their men. And they had an idea how to

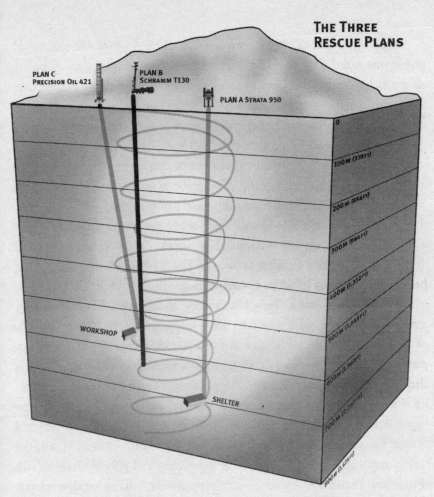

PLAN C
PRECISION OIL 421

PLAN B
SCHRAMM T130

PLAN A STRATA 950

0

100M (328FT)

200M (656FT)

300M (984FT)

400M (1,312FT)

500M (1,640FT)

600M (1,968FT)

700M (2,296FT)

800M (2,625FT)

WORKSHOP

SHELTER

get the equipment to the mine: They simply called UPS. Could the company carefully pack up seven heavy drills, make sure they didn't get lost, fly them to Copiapó—and do it for next to nothing?

If Plan A, the mining rig, was "The Turtle," Plan B, the percussion hammer water-well drill, was "The Rabbit." As Fisher explains, their drill is a "glorified jackhammer." The bottom of the drill keeps turning, while air-powered pistons raise and lower bits that smash into the rock. (This animation on the company site shows exactly how it works: centerrock.com/cri-in-action/low-profile-drill-action.) A drill may have four or more bits, and each of those is loaded with diamond inserts—the hardest substance in the world—so that they scrape and scour the ground. Other drills cut by turning, screwing down into the ground. This percussion hammer pounds as it turns.

Dr. Chavez explained that the drill has yet another advantage in old mines like the San José: If it breaks through to an abandoned mine tunnel it can keep going efficiently, whereas some other drills might overheat. So Plan B could work, but there was still one great unknown. Percussion hammer drills had previously only been used to drill straight down. Would they work in the tangled web of poorly mapped old diggings that was the San José?

As Roy Slack, head of Cementation, Inc. (which was running the Plan A drill) put it, Plan B was the "long shot." This was a new use of the percussion hammer drill on equipment Slack thought was not really the right size for the task. The Plan B crew was pushing their rig to "the extreme of its capability." There was every chance they would fail.

Fisher was not worried about failing; he knew he had to try. So when he got the okay from Chile, he left at once, reaching the mine by September 4. Geotech S. A., another worldwide mining company, had already gotten a Schramm T130XD drill to the mine and men to work it. Geotech, however, was more concerned, because no one at the mine had the slightest bit of experience widening a hole with the kind of equipment Fisher was bringing. They knew they needed help and they knew where to find it, half a world away.

Jeff Hart was about to take a very fast trip through the landscape of human history. He was in Southern Helmand Province in Afghanistan working with the army. Afghanistan has some of the oldest mines in the world. Six thousand years ago people were digging in those hills

	A	B	C	D	E	F	G
1			Gyroinclinometer				
2		Date: 27/08/2010					
3		Device Number: 63					
4		Crew: Geoatacama					
5		Operator: A. Mavrakis					
6		Well Number: 6C					
7		Field: San Jose					
8		Client: Minera San Esteban					
9		Well Depth: 0,00					
10							
11		Latitude: -27,15					
12		Magnetic Declination: 0,00					
13		Local Grid Offset: 0,00					
14		Starting Point Coordinates (in local grid):					
15		Northing: 0,00		Easting: 0,00		Altitude: 0,00	
16							
17		Description:					
18							
19		Azimuth measured in degrees and referenced to local grid					
20		Inclination measured from horizontal (up)					
21		Length measured in meters					
22							
		Depth	Azimuth	Angle			
25		0.0	195.47	-79.55			
26		10.0	194.08	-79.62			
27		20.0	195.16	-79.96			
30		380.0	198.00	-86.71			
31		390.0	199.52	-86.84			
32		400.0	203.59	-86.93			
33		410.0	206.59	-86.91			
34		420.0	209.17	-87.12			
35		430.0	211.75	-87.34			
36		440.0	215.49	-87.52			
37		450.0	217.01	-87.37			
38		460.0	219.44	-87.32			
39		470.0	221.87	-87.27			
40		480.0	223.56	-87.59			
41		490.0	225.07	-87.26			
42		500.0	225.07	-87.41			
43		510.0	225.07	-87.56			
44		520.0	228.19	-87.46			
45		530.0	231.12	-87.74			
46		540.0	230.97	-87.63			
47		550.0	229.24	-87.92			
48		560.0	232.36	-87.90			
49		570.0	232.30	-87.80			
50		580.0	226.71	-88.23			
51		590.0	229.02	-87.93			
52		600.0	232.59	-87.97			
53		610.0	231.87	-87.69			
54		620.0	231.03	-87.93			

6C_CM | Final Result | Sheet1

Normal View | Enter

This is the actual drilling log used by the Center Rock team. The first column shows depth in meters—their hole ended at 623 meters. The second column is the azimuth, the angle to the left or right. The third column shows the angle down. If they had been drilling straight down, that would be 90 degrees. The log shows how they started at an 11-degree angle and slowly straightened out, reaching 87.93, nearly vertical, as gravity took over. As Brandon Fisher explained, if you look at the azimuth column in the boxed area you can see where they had real problems: Between 390 and 400 meters down they quickly had to make a 4 percent change in direction turning left and then right (to view the path of the drill, see insert, page 6).

and finding the blue gems of lapis lazuli, as well as copper and gold. But the area has been crisscrossed with invasion and war so often since then that no one had ever gotten around to really studying the geology and soil. Jeff was there to dig down 1,500 feet to supply water wells for the soldiers while geologists were patiently mapping what lay beneath the brown hills. Being on a base, he could connect to the Internet and he had followed the story of the mine collapse so far away in Chile. "Obviously our interest was piqued," he told a reporter, "because it takes *drillers* to get the miners out. But never in our wildest dreams did we think they'd call us because it's too far away." And then on September 2, his cell phone rang.

Hart works for Layne Christensen Company, a drilling company. As he recalls, Geotech told his employer "we're in over our head.

Video brought ghostly images of the trapped men to the outside world.

We've never drilled anything this size with a hammer. We need to get some Layne guys in here and see what they can do." If this experiment was going to work they needed the men who knew how to get the most of the machines—no matter where they were.

Geotech had gotten the Schramm T130 rig to the site; Center Rock provided the percussion hammer drill to speed the way down; now they just needed Layne Christensen's expert drillers to man the machine. And so Jeff Hart and Matt Staffel were wanted on the phone, deep in Southern Helmand Province, Afghanistan.

A chartered jet whisked them to Dubai where they changed planes for Amsterdam, hopped over to Paris, and caught a flight to Santiago, Chile. After forty hours in the air they landed, just ten minutes after their Spanish-speaking colleagues Jorge Herrera and Doug Reeves, who had just jetted down from the United States. The four drillers raced off to Copiapó and the San José Mine.

Even as Jeff Hart was in the air, flying from Afghanistan, Fisher was speeding down to Chile. Back home the company was rushing to ready the support equipment. It took Center Rock five days to ready all seven drills. They needed to have so many both as backup in case one broke and so that they could keep cutting into the earth twenty-four hours a day. As Center Rock was building, UPS was planning. They figured out the most efficient, least expensive way to get the machines to the mine. No company was out to make money on the actual rescue—though good publicity is, well, good publicity. By 5:00 PM on Saturday, September 11, all of the drills Brandon was sure could save the men were in place at the San José Mine. But by then it was too late. Even as UPS was scrambling, disaster had struck at the mine.

At 879 feet down, the Center Rock drill shattered.

On September 9, the Plan B crew smashed into something. It turned out to be a steel bolt, a roof support from yet one more neglected and poorly described part of the mine. Parts of the drill were sheared off and dropped down. Pulling the broken drill back without further damage was hard enough, but the Plan B drill could not go back down until the crew got out the chunks of metal. Otherwise they would be sending down the next drill, only to get it chewed up by banging into its predecessor. It looked like the critics were right—too many things were likely to go wrong with the Center Rock drill. All work on Plan B stopped.

"WHEN ARE YOU GOING TO GET THEM OUT?"

The mood of the men below and the families in Camp Hope darkened. The Strata had finally reached down over 900 feet, but that still left nearly 1,400 to go. And it was scheduled to stop for repair and maintenance in a few days. There was talk of a massive Plan C drill, but it had not yet even arrived on the site. And now the one drill that had been zooming along, the Plan B team, lay in shattered and hard-to-retrieve pieces. Soon enough, instead of hearing the reassuring sounds of rescue drills above their heads, the trapped men would have only icy silence.

The one piece of good news came down one of the *paloma*s, which brought a special video to miner Ariel Ticona. The men knew to leave him alone as he watched it. The film showed his wife giving birth to their new baby daughter, whom they, of course, named Esperanza—"Hope."

Fisher and his team did not take the broken drill as a tragedy. They just needed to get a magnet, fish out the shrapnel, and start again. As Jeff Hart walked up the hill at the mine, the very first thing he saw was the broken drill hammer laid out, waiting to be examined. That just meant he needed to get to work, joining Fisher in cleaning out the hole so they could drill again.

Location, figuring out exactly where and how to drill to reach a tiny target far underground, had been Kelvin Brown's problem when he was dealing with old maps, and it would be Hart's and Staffel's as well. Hart's voice gets louder when he speaks about the driller's challenge: "Everything we do, we do blind." That is why he is so passionate about math—everyday school math. Calculating the depth they have reached, the weight of the drill, the angle of entry, and the slope of the hole is the only way they could ever succeed. And that was especially true at San José. The mine was so old and crisscrossed with abandoned tunnels that they had to come in from the side: That hole began at eleven degrees off vertical and needed to end up two degrees off. "We went back to basic math," Jeff explained. They needed to lay out the path they would need to travel by figuring out "if we're starting at this angle" how they needed to bend and "come back to true vertical, and actually hit that point in the mine."

Hart and Staffel were supposed to drill in twelve-hour shifts, so that the process would keep going, just as Brandon Fisher and Richard Soppe were meant to spell each other in troubleshooting the drill bits. But it didn't work that way—the rhythm of the drilling was determined by whatever current crisis they faced. Whenever a problem arose, and they did often, everyone helped out, then someone dashed off for a three- or four-hour nap, until the next crisis. Every three or four days someone got lucky enough to leave the camp and take a shower.

Sixteen days into the drilling, Julie Fisher came over to join her husband and serve as "mother, sister, friend"—making coffee, answering phones, and keeping the team afloat.

The Fishers' cots were set up in a rectangular, metal shipping container—their temporary home. Looking out her window, Mrs. Fisher could now see three rigs: Plan A, the Strata 950 pounding away; Plan B, the Schramm T130 with her husband's drill heads; and the third contestant, Plan C, Precision Drilling's 421 oil drilling rig.

PLAN C: THE TRANSFORMER

The giant had finally arrived—to great fanfare. For here was the heavyweight, the insurance plan, the mammoth Precision Rig-421 drill that would reach the men no matter what.

When the forty-three trucks carrying parts of the rig were driven to the site they paraded through Camp Hope, greeted with cheers. "The Transformer," it was soon nicknamed since it came in parts that assembled into a giant, began work on September 19. A dozen Canadians were running the 141-foot-tall titan, keeping the same hours as the other two crews. This was a race—but the prize was saving human lives. Every night when Shaun Robstad, the rig's field supervisor, called to his family just outside of Calgary, his eleven-year-old daughter would ask, "When are you going to get them out?"

When indeed. The Strata started first, but was very slow. The 421 oil rig didn't need a pilot hole, but, like the Plan B Schramm, it had to go in on one angle and then shift to another to avoid old tunnels. That left it to the long shot, the little drill that could, as long as they did not hit any more steel surprises.

There are only two ways to know what is happening where your drill bit cuts the earth, explained Hart. You use math, and you use your feet. An experienced driller cannot watch from the side and let a machine grind on. He has to stand up the whole time and feel the vibrations. He has to sense when there is good torque, as the drill head makes solid contact and bites through the earth, and when there is bad torque, as the machine is binding, and he has to act fast to prevent another disaster.

On the work site, the shifts were blurring into one another; every team was running twenty-four-hour days. The mood in the camp

Brandon Fisher, left, and Richard Soppe, kneeling next to the Center Rock drill that dug the escape shaft for the miners.

improved. On September 18, the Plan B drill finished drilling its first hole, widening the space from five inches to twelve. As the drill pulled out, rock tumbled down below, where the miners were ready. Clearing out that pile of rubble was just one more chore, one more step they could take to lead them to freedom. The next day the twenty-eight-inch drill began working its way down to the men.

On September 25, the first of the rescue capsules arrived on the site. Navarro and his team had done their work, and given their creation the perfect name: Phoenix. The capsule would rise from the ground, bringing life, just as the mythical bird was reborn in fire. The Phoenix was also a sign that the actual rescue was due to start soon. Three days later the Plan B drill got past the area where it had previously smashed into the steel bolt and was down to 987 feet.

On October 4, the Plan B drill stood at 1,532 feet. A last glitch—the final angle was too tight, so Hart and Staffel decided they needed to switch to a twenty-six-inch head. But they had always known this might happen. Twenty-six inches was still wide enough for the Phoenix. The Plan A crew now realized that their hole would not be needed and indeed could be a danger to the miners as water that had built up in the open cavity would cascade down on them, so they stopped work four days away from reaching the men.

In this version of the story, the rabbit beat the turtle and the titan. The risk, the mix of Fisher's confidence and Hart's know-how, was about to pay off.

On October 9, the Center Rock drill reached 2,040 feet, and crashed through to the men. The channel was clear. Julie and Richard Brandon "went down to Camp Hope and hugged many of the family members, there were tears of joy from both them and us." Then the entire drilling crew left the camp to make room for the Phoenix team. The final moment would belong to the miners and their families.

On October 11, special, thin steel plates were attached to the first 350 feet of the shaft, so no loose rocks could harm the rising miners.

The men had been trapped in a neglected mine, saved by themselves, and found by an Australian and his team of South Africans and Chileans. Canadians and Americans had raced down to free them, and now, if the Phoenix could fly, they would return home, safe.

CHAPTER TWELVE

PHOENIX RISING

PHOENIX

The men had been trapped for sixty-nine days, the entire world was watching, nothing could go wrong. Captain Navarro and his team needed to think of everything. What must, absolutely must, be in the rescue capsule? What would a miner need if everything was going well, if a few things went wrong, or if there was a disaster? What kinds of physical, medical, or even mental accidents could take place? How could they be prevented or overcome? Who should leave the mine first, and who last?

The Chileans reviewed NASA's suggestions and made use of many of them. For example, adding oxygen tanks and communication devices to the capsules. Nearly two-thirds of astronauts who have been stuck in the cramped quarters of space capsules faint when they first stand up. What if a miner fainted in the Phoenix? His heart might not be able to get enough blood to his brain. Dr. Benjamin Levine, a University of Texas professor who works with NASA, suggested the men wear compression stockings—special socks that would raise their blood pressure, and be trained to cough as they rose, pushing blood to the brain.

The men were to be dressed in clothes made of Hipora, a synthetic fabric that is waterproof and will allow sweat to go through it. They already had biometric belts that could monitor blood pressure, body temperature, and breathing rate, and beam the data by Bluetooth to a watching doctor's screen. Jonathan Franklin, a reporter for the British newspaper the *Guardian*, contacted the Oakley company out of concern for the men's vision. Oakley donated thirty-five

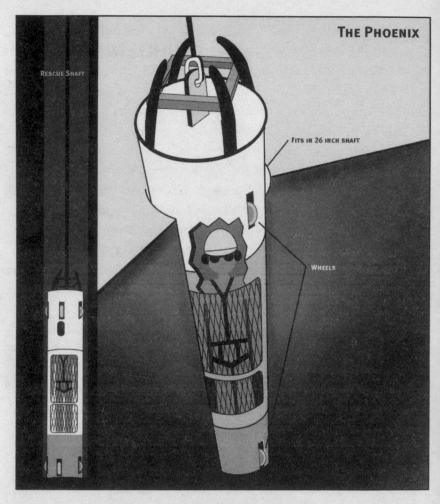

RESCUE SHAFT

FITS IN 26 INCH SHAFT

WHEELS

top-of-the-line wraparound sunglasses so that the men, whose eyes had grown accustomed to darkness, would not be blinded by the light. To speed them on their way, every man wore one of the blue bracelets with the white number 33 on it that Julie Fisher had brought with her when she joined her husband, Brandon, on the site. A special winch invented in Austria had been set up at the mine to carefully raise the capsule from beneath the ground.

In movies and novels, it is always women and children—the most vulnerable people—who are rescued first. After all, that seems to be the noble thing to do. But Captain Navarro knew that would be a mistake. If anything went wrong in the Phoenix, it should be the strongest, most alert miner who had to fight his way out. The first set of miners who tested the system had to be in good shape. Only once everyone knew there were no problems could the weaker men rise. But who should have the honor—the men clearly saw it that way—of going last? The last miner must again be fit and alert—he was the only one who might have no backup. Unless a rescue squad went down to help, if he slipped and fell unconscious, the nearest person would be two thousand feet away. But the last man must also be the person who deserved to be seen as the captain, the leader who stayed with his men until the entire crew was safe.

This test run showed how the Phoenix capsule would slowly rise to the waiting world.

Dr. Iturra suggested that the rescue begin very early, since the airport at Copiapó sometimes gets fogged-in by the afternoon. He wanted all the men on their way to the hospital as fast as possible, no time for air-traffic delays. That was the level of detail and care—every step was reviewed and improved before it was approved.

OCTOBER 13 RISING

Just after midnight, a siren sounds and a cable is pulling something out of a hole, like a fishing line hauling in a big catch. A ring of four

Mario Gómez, the oldest miner and spiritual counselor to his fellow men, tastes the open air for the first time in sixty-nine days.

OPPOSITE: Though Edison Peña needed to be carried in a stretcher after he reached safety, he had trained so well down in the mine that he managed to complete the New York Marathon less than a month later.

metal brackets, like a folded-in crown, emerges. Behind it slowly glides a cylinder that looks like a thin space capsule. It is as if a rocket is launching in slow motion. The capsule is painted in three sections: the white, blue, then red of the Chilean flag. Children in white hard hats wait. President Piñera waits. The capsule—this missile sent up from the depths of the Earth—arrives, lands. A cluster of helpers gathers at the door. "Chi Chi Chi Le Le Le! Los mineros de Chile!" chants the crowd. Florencio Avalos emerges, red hat, light on the top, clean shaven, pauses. Then hugs, and hugs, and hugs . . .

The Phoenix rides start slowly, but move along more quickly as all goes smoothly. One by one by one the capsules are rising, the bird is flying, the men are coming home.

At 9:55 PM, the siren wails again and the cable is pulling. The crown, then the capsule, arises, steadies, lands, and Luis Urzúa—the shift captain, the man who earned the honor of being last—emerges. The president holds him; they embrace. It is over. The world rescued the men. In turn, the men gave an example to the world.

THE HOLLOW EARTH

THE RESCUE OF THE THIRTY-THREE was a triumph for Chile. Its ministers and doctors, engineers and miners were experienced, level-headed, and intelligent about their needs and in touch with the world, ready and able to accept help. The story of San José is also a triumph for the skills and tools now used in mining. It shows what we can do now to read the world beneath our feet, and bring back its treasures safely. Miners in China watched and learned, seeing how their work could be safer. Individuals and companies from Australia, Austria, Canada, Japan, South Africa, South Korea, the United States—everyone from experts on undersea and underground to outer space—helped out.

The miners had the benefit of the latest technology and information: fiber-optic cables, biometric belts, Hipora clothing, cell phone projectors, state of the art knowledge of nutrition, NASA's best studies of how to plan the routines of the men and the emotions of their families. The best drills and drillers rushed from more than half a world away to help out. And yet the most important reason the men came home safe was how they behaved when they were totally alone. In those seventeen days when they were isolated, they chose their leader, pulled together, and worked for their own rescue. They did what they could, even though they had no idea if that would make any difference. The lost men trusted in one another and in their faith, and made the best of every moment. Those skills were as valuable in the bottom of a mine with no equipment as they were in the fullest possible glare of the world's attention. From the bottom of the earth, they set an example for us.

One of the strangest theories about the underground world was the idea that Earth was hollow. For some wild reason this theory was popular in the 1800s, and even among believers in the 1900s. The idea was that there were entrances to the Earth at the poles, and some kind of secret, advanced civilization deep inside the planet. Some even believed that all of us are actually inside the world, looking up at a sun that is the planet's core. There is one sense in which the story of the thirty-three almost fits that belief.

We are all trapped together on this multibillion-year-old planet. As Dr. Martin Luther King Jr. wrote, "We are caught in an inescapable network of mutuality, tied in a single garment of destiny. Whatever affects one directly, affects all indirectly." It is easy to feel good about pitching in to help these men, but we all constantly use the products of mines without thinking about how we get them.

This is a book about a successful mine rescue, but that happy ending came through lessons learned in so many other accidents— at Quecreek, in Tasmania, and around the globe. Just over a month after the Phoenix completed its last run, twenty-nine men were killed in a coal mine in New Zealand. Mining is a dangerous job that makes all of our lives better. We cannot be like those ancient Greeks who proudly waved the swords of Hephaistos, while making fun of the men who forged them.

The metals and minerals we use every day link us to the men who go down into the earth to find them. Their safety and well-being is our safety and well-being. The whole world helped the miners in Chile, but that great rescue will have been wasted if we go back to buying the products of unsafe mines because we are so happy to have a slightly cheaper product from a mine that decided not to spend money on escape routes or new maps. We need to be as alert to those who practice good mining as we are to those who run healthier farms or better factories. When we behave like Urzúa's miners we can survive, we can pull through, we can rise. In that sense they were outside and we were down below—and they can help us see the way out. We can all be "well in our shelter" so long as we care for it, and for one another. If we want the treasures of the Earth, we need to value our miners, not just when they are trapped by rocks, but whenever they enter the kingdom of the dark.

MORE INFORMATION ABOUT THE MINERS can be found at king5.com/home/related/Bios-of-all-33-miners-104839004.html and elsewhere on the Web. I have added only a few notes about men with similar names and the individuals I featured in the book.

Claudio Acuña—35

Juan Carlos Aguilar—49

Osmán Araya—30

Florencio Ávalos—31

Renán Ávalos—29. Florencio is his brother.

Samuel Ávalos—43

Carlos Barrios—27

Yonni Barrios—50. He helped out with medical issues underground.

Carlos Bugueño—27

Raúl Bustos—40

Pedro Cortez—26

Jorge Galleguillos—56

Mario Gómez—64. The oldest miner, he also became the spiritual leader underground.

José Henríquez—54

Daniel Herrera—27

Juan Illanes—52

Franklin Lobos—52. A former soccer player turned copper miner.

Carlos Mamani—24. The only miner from Bolivia.

José Ojeda—48

Edison Peña—34. He helped arrange lighting underground, and trained to run in the New York Marathon—which he completed less than a month after he was rescued.

Omar Reygadas—56

Esteban Rojas—44

Pablo Rojas—45. Esteban's brother.

Jimmy Sánchez—19

Darío Segovia—39

Víctor Segovia—48

Mario Sepúlveda—40. He became one of the leaders, and was the second miner to be rescued.

Ariel Ticona—24

Luis Urzua—54. The shift captain and last man to be rescued. Along with Sepúlveda and Gómez, he led the men underground.

Álex Vega—31

Richard Villarroel—28

Claudio Yáñez—34

Víctor Zamora—33

TIMELINE

August 5, 2010—A cave-in at the San José Mine traps thirty-three
   miners 2,300 feet belowground.

August 7—One hundred and thirty rescue workers are at work at the
   mine. But a second cave-in forces the rescue team to the surface,
   making a quick rescue unlikely. Laurence Golborne, the Chilean
   government's minister of Mining and Energy, tells reporters that
   "the easiest, most logical way in is now blocked. Experts are going
   to have to find other alternatives, but those will be tougher and take
   longer." Far below, Mario Gómez and Mario Sepúlveda organize
   the trapped men.

August 9—Three hundred people are now gathered at the site—a
   mix of family, friends, fellow miners, engineers, experts, and
   government ministers.

August 10 (St. Lawrence day)—The bishop of Copiapó, Caspar
   Quintana, holds a mass at the mine on this Catholic feast day.

August 14—The miners' rations have dwindled to just a bite of
   canned tuna for each man every thirty-six hours.

August 15—Kelvin Brown and the Reflex Instruments drill arrive in
   Copiapó.

August 10–21—Nine drills, arrayed in an arc around the mine, drive
   down toward the trapped miners.

August 21—With just two days of food left, the thirty-three survive on two hundred calories a day; they have each lost nearly fifteen pounds.

August 22—The Schramm T685 drill bit crashes through the ceiling of the trapped miners' shelter. The miners tape to the drill a bag with two letters, including José Ojeda's message to the world: *Estamos bien en el refugio los 33* ("We are in the shelter and are well, the 33").

August 23—The thirty-three begin receiving fresh supplies as three new steel-lined holes are drilled to the shelter.

August 27—Video images of the miners are seen for the first time.

August 31—A Strata 950 drilling rig (Plan A), brought in from a nearby mine, begins drilling a possible rescue shaft.

September 4—Brandon Fisher arrives and is soon followed by Jeff Hart.

September 9—The Center Rock, Inc., percussion hammer drill (Plan B) shatters after hitting a steel bolt 879 feet below the surface.

September 18—The Plan B drill finishes its first hole, widening the space from five inches to twelve.

September 19—The Precision Rig-421 drill (Plan C) begins drilling.

September 28—The Plan B drill pushes down to 987 feet, past the area where it had previously shattered.

October 4—The Plan B drill reaches 1,532 feet. Seeing the Center Rock team close to reaching the miners, the Plan A team stops drilling.

October 9—The Plan B drill breaks through to the miners.

October 13—Beginning just after midnight, the thirty-three are brought one by one to the surface in the Phoenix capsule. Luis Urzúa emerges last at 9:55 PM.

GLOSSARY

René Aguilar—A risk management expert from El Teniente, sent to the mine to plan the logistics of the rescue operation.

Andes—The longest mountain range in the world. It stretches across the west coast of South America, and is located in the countries of Chile, Argentina, Peru, Bolivia, Venezuela, Colombia, and Ecuador.

Aphrodite—In Greek mythology, she is the goddess of love and beauty.

Ares—In Greek mythology, he is the god of war and bravery.

Atacama Desert—Located in northern Chile, it is considered the driest desert in the world.

Atacama Fault—A place where the Nazca and South American tectonic plates meet. Collision and rubbing of these plates creates earthquakes.

Fidel Baez—The project manager of the San José Mine rescue operation.

Bluetooth—A technology used in computers, cellular phones, and other devices as a form of short-range wireless communication.

bore—The inside diameter of a hole or drill bit.

brass—An alloy (metal combination) of copper and zinc that looks like dirty gold.

Bronze Age—A time in history during which a given group of people use bronze (a combination of tin and copper) as their primary tool and weapon material.

Kelvin Brown—A drilling consultant and product manager from Australian company Reflex Instruments.

Camp Hope—The name of the makeshift town surrounding the San José Mine. The camp included journalists, family members of the miners, and rescue personnel.

Cementation, Inc.—The Canadian mining company that supplied the drill used for Plan A.

Center Rock, Inc.—A Pennsylvania-based company that provided drill bits for Plan B and engineering assistance for the Copiapó mine rescue.

Dr. William Chavez—A professor of mineral exploration and engineering from the New Mexico Institute of Mining and Technology.

CODELCO—The copper company that operates the Copiapó mine

Copiapó—A mining city in northern Chile, located in the Atacama Desert. The mines surrounding this town have large gold and copper deposits.

Clint Cragg—A NASA engineer who drafted the design criteria for the Phoenix rescue capsule.

Death Valley—A desert valley in southern California. It is the hottest desert in the northern hemisphere.

Demeter—In Greek mythology, she is the goddess of the field harvest. According to the mythology, her journeys to and from Hades regulated the four seasons of the year.

Dr. Michael Duncan—He headed the team of NASA experts who came to help out in the rescue.

Thomas Alva Edison—The New Jersey innovator who created the lightbulb, the phonograph, the motion picture camera, and the direct current (DC) transmission line.

Gene Fallon—An employee of Cementation, Inc., who monitored Plan A.

feldspar—A kind of mineralized rock. This kind of rock is often made as lava flow cools.

Brandon Fisher—Founder and president of Center Rock, Inc., and husband of Julie Fisher.

Julie Fisher—Sales director for Center Rock, Inc., and wife of Brandon Fisher.

Tom Foy—A worker at Center Rock, Inc.

UPS—An acronym for United Parcel Service, an international shipping company.

Captain Renato Navarro Genta—The commander of a Chilean navy unit called "Task Group 33," which helped keep the trapped miners physically and psychologically fit.

Geotech—A South American drilling company whose drill was used to create an escape route for the miners.

Laurence Golborne—The Chilean government's minister of Mining and Energy.

Hades—In Greek mythology, he is the god of the dead who also shares the same name as the Greek underworld.

Jeff V. Hart—The head operator of the Plan B drilling operation.

Hephaistos— In Greek mythology, he is the god of metal, creative art, fire, and volcanoes; he was also lame and often portrayed as ugly or disfigured.

Himalayas—The world's tallest mountain range.

Dr. Albert (Al) Holland—A psychologist from NASA who used his expertise in astronaut psychology to keep the rescue team and trapped miners mentally organized and calm.

Humboldt Current—An ocean current system that flows from the southern tip of Chile to northern Peru.

igneous rock—A type of rock formed from magma or lava. Pumice, granite, and obsidian are types of igneous rock.

Kristian Jahn—A Chilean official who gathered psychologists who could comfort the trapped miners' families.

Layne Christensen Company—A drilling company that operated the drill for Plan B.

Dr. Benjamin Levine—A University of Texas professor who works at NASA as a person who researches ways to keep astronauts comfortable in space.

Ron Mishkin—A mining historian and former worker at the Sterling Hill mine.

NASA—An acronym for the National Aeronautics and Space Administration, the U. S. agency in charge of the country's space program.

Nazca Plate—An underwater tectonic plate that runs along the Chilean sea border.

Orpheus—A person from Greek mythology who had the power to control people, animals, and objects using music.

Osiris—A god from Egyptian mythology who ruled the underworld and the souls who resided there.

Padre Negro—Meaning "Black Father," this little village outside of Copiapó was once a barracks where Spanish conquistadors (soldiers) kept their slave laborers that worked the mines. Now it is a small village for mine workers who cannot afford to buy their own homes.

paloma—"Pigeon" in the Spanish language. This name was given to the small capsules that delivered food, water, and other items to the miners trapped in the San José Mine.

President Piñera—The leader of Chile who took office shortly before the mine rescue.

Dr. J. D. Polk—Chief of Space Medicine at the Johnson Space Center. He brought his knowledge of emergency evacuations to the mine.

Potosí—A Bolivian city that is located next to a gigantic silver mine.

Reflex Instruments—A company that provided surveying instruments that helped plan the miners' rescue.

Shaun Robstad—The superintendent of a Canadian company called Precision Drilling.

San José—"Saint José," the name of the mine that collapsed on August 5, 2010.

Andre Sougarret—An engineer from El Teniente and the University of Chile who helped plan the mine rescue.

Sterling Hill Mine—Located in Ogdensburg, New Jersey. It was first founded as a copper mine and was the last functioning underground mine in the state when it closed in 1986. It was turned into a museum in 1990.

TauTona and **Savuka**—Two gold mines in South Africa; TauTona is the deepest mining operation in the world.

tectonic plate—A large piece of the Earth's crust. When tectonic plates collide or rub against one another, the result is an earthquake.

Amerigo Vespucci—An Italian mapmaker and navigator who explored South America from 1499 to 1502. It is most likely that the continents of North and South America were named after him.

Yost Drilling—A Pennsylvania drilling company that helped to drill rescue shafts at several North American coal mines.

THE WORLD OF THE MINER

BY RON MISHKIN

MINERS ARE A BREED APART. I can say that because I am a former underground hard rock miner in zinc and copper mines and a geologist in iron mines. We work in damp, dark, dirty, dangerous, and claustrophobic conditions that can range from extremely hot and humid in the mines of Arizona to freezing in the high mountain mines of Colorado. One of the worst fears many people have is being buried alive. Miners must overcome that fear while working hundreds or even thousands of feet underground in the tight chambers of the mine.

Most hard rock (metal) mines are deep and steep so miners must climb muddy ladders through nearly vertical openings, or "raises," to go from one level to another. A raise may be three hundred feet high—so even though you are deep underground, you now have to overcome a fear of falling.

A miner must be acutely aware of his working environment at all times and must be sure to perform his tasks perfectly. He must bar down all loose overhead rock and install rock bolts. Leaving a loose chunk overhead is an invitation to disaster. He must be sure no unexploded dynamite remains in the muck pile after a blast. A friend in my carpool was killed in a horrible accident. He was crushed by a five-ton chunk of magnetite while setting up a blast.

With all of these hazards and consequences, why would anyone choose to be a miner? Miners are a brotherhood of guys who love the adventure of it. They are great practical jokers and love busting chops. Like nailing your lunch box to a plank or placing a peanut butter and grease sandwich in your lunch box. And miners like being miners. They have a lot of pride in what they do, because they realize the rest of us could never do this job. It helps that the pay is very good. For all of the dangers, in a way, miners are stress free. They get to wear crummy clothes, drill holes in solid rock, swear all day, blast the ore down, and go home whistling.

Miners know that they are providing the resources that make the wheels of civilization turn. Without mining we would be back in the Stone Age. In fact, I believe the men who go down into the Earth are heroes. Their willingness to descend into the black depths and wrest minerals from the unforgiving Earth makes our way of life possible.

Ron Mishkin has had extensive experience in underground mining, working first as a miner in zinc and copper mines, then as a mining geologist in iron mines and as a consultant to the industry.

HOW I WROTE THIS BOOK
AND WHAT I LEARNED THAT COULD BE USEFUL FOR
STUDENTS WRITING RESEARCH REPORTS (AND A
COUPLE OF LAST THOUGHTS FROM MEN I INTERVIEWED)

I HAVE WRITTEN BOOKS about politicians who were popular when I was growing up (Robert Kennedy, for example) and even people alive today (Bill Gates), but this is the first book I've written about a current event. I learned a lot. In all of my other books, I could begin by reading, well, books. Someone else had filtered the news reports, dug through the sources, conducted the interviews. Indeed, in nearly every case, those first books had themselves been reviewed, questioned, and critiqued, and new, improved, even competing interpretations had been published. So when I began my research I had that library of prior work to use as my foundation. As I'll explain in a moment, I still believe reading existing books is the best place to begin your own research, but for *Trapped* I had to use a different strategy. When I began, I knew of one book that was due to come out in a few months—but I couldn't wait. I finally got to read Jonathan Franklin's book *33 Men* only as this one was already in production. I had to build my book up from what I could find on the Internet or learn in interviews. In a sense, then, I was closer to the experience of most students than when I have a full academic library at my back.

Every time I visit a school to help students with their research reports, the same thing happens: Once I finish my talk, they scatter to the computers and race to Google. In crafting this book that is what I, like Brandon Fisher when he was building his case to the Chilean government, had to do. I learned something interesting.

The main problem with the Internet as a resource is not that it has inaccurate information. Of course it does, and Wikipedia, the number one landing place on many search lists, sometimes does. The largest problem with researching on the Net is that it gives you a false sense of bounty—as if there were so much there a keystroke away. The real gems of the Net do not show up in convenient order on a search page. You only find them when you know what questions to ask.

The sources that come up first and are easiest to find are, well, thin and flat. That is, they repeat, and repeat, and repeat the same information. For example, it was very easy to find an article about Jeff Hart, the driller who completed the shaft that freed the miners. In fact the very same article, with the same photo, was passed around from one paper to another, filling up page after page of Google search. There was a nice YouTube video of his TV appearance, but it added nothing new to that same story. A bit deeper in the search, the articles began to take on a political tinge, as conservatives and liberals made use of his story. But that was not the problem. I needed to know more than that single repeated paragraph. For example, not one article listed the actual date on which he got the call in Afghanistan, nor how he first heard of the mine collapse. Only on the fourth page of my Google listing did I find a longer article, from the online journal of the American Water Works Association, which began to fill in the blanks in Hart's story. Indeed, the sequence of events as reported in *33 Men* is incorrect.

The first thing you learn in journalism class is to ask the five key questions: who, what, when, where, and why. If you begin with those questions, then the Net can help you. But you will have to cut through the underbrush of articles that rush to repeat what other articles say. Those articles are released on deadline; their job is to give readers something, a taste, a sound bite of information. But a book, like a research report, is after something else—not a quick look-see, but deeper knowledge. And you can only find that on the Net if you are the driver.

Take the stories of what happened in the mine during those seventeen days before the drill broke through to the shelter. Obviously they only began to emerge after the miners were found, and, most often, after they were back home. So I had to read in two different timelines: day-by-day articles during the disaster to learn what people knew as events unfolded, and then after-the-fact articles in which miners looked back and talked about what they had experienced. There are useful leads to all of those in the main Wikipedia entry, but there you are following the trail left by whoever compiled that story. And then your work will merely be a smaller summary of Wikipedia's summary—the story of the mine getting, well, thinner and flatter as it passes from hand to hand.

The great advantage of books is that the knowledge in them has been cooked. Someone had the time to think about what he or she wanted to say and how best to say it. That is why, whenever possible, students should read enough in a book to head out to the Net with a beginning sense of what they want to know. Armed with their own passions, their own curiosities, and their own list of specific questions, they will quickly see when they are getting the same stuff rehashed and repeated, and when they have found something new. As I always say in schools, no one would ever begin a shopping trip by Googling the word "clothes"—you would always start out with a sense of the style, price, and even store you have in mind. The same is true of doing research—the more you already know when you turn on the computer the more the Net can do for you.

Being a journalist was thrilling, especially when I got to speak with people like Kelvin Brown, Dr. Holland, Jeff Hart, and Brandon and Julie Fisher, who were actually part of the events at the San José Mine. That is something I don't get to do when, say, writing about the Salem witch trials. The Net makes it very easy to find people, and students may well have the opportunity to do their own interviews. Speaking from the other side, though, as an author students have contacted, I appreciate it when they come with good questions after having done previous research. Asking me to summarize my book is insulting. Asking me about something in a book—even strongly disagreeing with a point I've made—is a sign of engagement and respect. Come to an interview as an informed reporter and the person you are speaking to may well give you fresh insights you cannot get anywhere else.

Finally, two of the men I interviewed had ideas they wanted to pass along to young readers. Jeff Hart speaks in many schools, and always about the same thing: math. Math is not a set of tests and problems you get through because you have to. It is a language that allows people like him to hit a target blind, thousands of feet away, to save lives, to bring water to our troops. He suspects that people who drill into the Earth use more math than any other profession. Math matters.

Dr. Holland has some advice to any young person who wants to be an astronaut, who wants to be part of that historic team that will go to Mars and beyond: You must read, a lot. Read about people who were in extreme circumstances, like Ernest Shakleton and his crew. Read about those who survived, and those who didn't. Study what skills allowed men and women to do the impossible, to rise to a challenge, and what held them back. If you want to go out into space, learn from the men deep in the mine.

NOTES AND SOURCES

I HAVE LIMITED the citations listed here to sources of actual quotations and details not generally available from other articles and reports. Students interested in learning more should start with Jennifer Yang's summary article and Jonathan Franklin's series of articles in the *Guardian* and *Washington Post*, as well as his book *33 Men*.

CHAPTER ONE

p. 3 Jennifer Yang, *Toronto Star* (October 10, 2010).

CHAPTER TWO

p. 8 Simon Lamb, *Devil in the Mountain*, pages 302–305. See also geo.arizona.edu/geo5xx/geo527/Andes/intro.html and geo. arizona.edu/geo5xx/geo527/Andes/Magmandes.html for interviews and discussions that show there are scientists who disagree with Lamb's theory. Lamb's book is an expert geologist's effort to reach a wider adult audience by combining personal travel with speculations on how the Andes were formed.

p. 11 Ron Mishkin, interview by author (December 2010).

p. 11 Onofre Tafoya, *Mother Magma*, page 6.

p. 13 Dr. William Chavez, interview by author (December 2010).

CHAPTER THREE

p. 14 For more on Maund's observations on Chile, see news.goldseek .com/CliveMaund/1287072563.php. Maund's comment on page 10 is from an interview by the author (December 2010).

pp. 14, 16 For a description of Padre Negro, see Franklin Briceno and Eva Vegara, the Associated Press (October 17, 2010); for Chavez, see Chavez interview.

p. 16 For more on Vega, see CNN Wire Staff, CNN (August 31, 2010); for more on Gómez, see Andrew Gregory, *Mirror* (August 28, 2010).

p. 17 For the early history of metalwork, and more generally for historical background, see Martin Lynch, *Mining in World History*, page 10. This is a readable summary of mining activities and processes around the world. Any students wanting to do further research on mining should consult it as a reference.

p. 17 Rick Riordan, *The Lightning Thief*, page 242.

p. 17 For Hephaistos, Adrienne Mayor of Stanford led me to Dr. Willam Hansen, who generously supplied me with leads, as did Dr. Lora Holland. The views mentioned in the text are, of course, my own.

p. 20 For the spread of bronze see Kristian Kristiansen and Thomas B. Larsson, *The Rise of Bronze Age Society*, pages 110–12. This is a dense and highly theoretical work written for specialists, but its key insight is easy to grasp: The Bronze Age was nothing like our usual image of the "ancient world." It was not an era of farming settlements on which people stayed in their ancestral lands and did the same work in the same ways for centuries. Instead it was an era with great movements of peoples, exchanges of goods and ideas—a period of active change, not settled routine. One of the archaeologists I met at Stonehenge recommended it to me as the best current thinking on the Bronze Age.

p. 20 For more on electricity and new copper processes, see Lynch, pages 176–80.

CHAPTER FOUR

p. 21 For "the assessment," see *Pakistan Observer* (August 7, 2010); for "We hope," see *Irish Times* (August 6, 2010).

p. 22 For "There is a shelter," see ABC News (Australia Broadcasting Company), (August 6, 2010).

p. 22 For "personally promised," see Alonso Soto, Reuters (August 8, 2010).

p. 22 For "It was always," see Jonathan Franklin, *Guardian* (August 25, 2010).

p. 24 For "Murderers" and "his voice," see Alonso Soto, Reuters (August 7, 2010).

p. 24 For more on the experts sent from El Teniente, see Jennifer Yang, *Toronto Star* (October 16, 2010).

p. 24 For "saw rocks falling," see Graeme Culliford, *Mirror* (October 17, 2010).

p. 25 For more on Sepúlveda, see Jonathan Franklin, *33 Men*, pages 53, 56–60.

p. 25 For "very protective," see *Mirror* (October 14, 2010); for "We always say," see Jonathan Franklin, *Guardian* (October 14, 2010); for "every accident," see Mishkin, interview; for "The only thing we could do," see Culliford, *Mirror* (October 17, 2010).

p. 26 For "knew otherwise," see *Telegraph* (October 14, 2010).

p. 26 For "to let my family," see Culliford, *Mirror* (October 17, 2010).

p. 26 For "We were waiting," see Jonathan Franklin and Juan Forero, *The Washington Post* (October 15, 2010).

p. 27 For "You just have to speak," see Jonathan Franklin and Rory 27, *Guardian* (October 14, 2010).

p. 27 For "We talked about it," see Franklin and Carroll, *Guardian* (October 14, 2010).

p. 27 For more on the value of eating together, see Kathy Kristof, "Chilean Miners: Leadership Lessons from Luis Urzúa," moneywatch.bnet.com/saving-money/blog/devil-details/chilean-miners-leadership-lessons-from-luis-urzua/3142.

p. 28 For the amount of food, see Franklin, *33 Men*, page 24; for the water, see Franklin, *33 Men*, page 61.

CHAPTER FIVE

p. 29 For "I know it may," see Soto, Reuters (August 8, 2010).

p. 29 For "I'm not the kind of person," see Wire Staff, CNN.com (August 31, 2010).

p. 30 For "We have gone from hours," see Alonso Soto, Reuters (August 9, 2010).

p. 31 For more on religion at the mine site, see *Adventist Review* (October 20, 2010) and Rory Carroll, *Guardian* (October 11, 2010).

p. 32 For "The situation is very complex," see *Earth Times* (August 10, 2010).

p. 32 For "This is not easy," see Agence France Press (August 8, 2010).

p. 32 For Baez, see Yang, *Toronto Star* (October 10, 2010).

p. 34 For Chavez, see Chavez, interview; for Mishkin, see Mishkin, interview.

p. 36 For "white butterfly," see Rory Carroll, *Guardian*, (October 11, 2010).

p. 36 For "When the noise" and "The really great," see Wright Thompson, ESPN.com.

p. 37 For "We worked hard," see Jonathan Franklin and Juan Forero, *The Washington Post* (October 12, 2010).

CHAPTER SIX

p. 38 For "human gold," see Kelvin Brown, Lilian Gómez, et al, "Entombed," interview by Michael Usher, September 10, 2010, *60 Minutes*.

p. 38 For "Everyone was trying," and more on the Brown interview, see Jennifer Yang, *Toronto Star* (October 10, 2010); for details on the control room, see Kelvin Brown, interview by author (September 10, 2010).

p. 39 For "had not been updated," see Philip Sherwell, *Telegraph* (August 28, 2010).

p. 40 For "I wasn't prepared," see Brown, interview.

p. 42 For "After several days" and for the report of more air below, see Brown, interview.

p. 42 For more on the changing rations, see Franklin, *33 Men*, page 102.

p. 42 For "the probes were," see Franklin and Forero, *Guardian* (October 14, 2010); for "This hell," see Culliford, *Mirror* (October 17, 2010).

p. 42 For "take care of your mother," see Franklin, *33 Men*, page 111.

pp. 42–43 For more on the immovable rock, see Brown, interview.

p. 43 For "told us to have strength" and "we started to eat," see Franklin and Forero, *Guardian* (October 14, 2010).

CHAPTER SEVEN

p. 44 For more on dwindling food sources, see Franklin, *33 Men*, page 116.

p. 44 For "We were all waiting," see Simon Gardner and Terry Wade, Reuters (October 19, 2010).

p. 44 For "It was getting" and "a powder keg," see Yang, *Toronto Star* (October 16, 2010).

p. 45 For "softer material," *Stirling Times* (October 18, 2010).

PART TWO
CHAPTER EIGHT

p. 51 For more on Urzúa's exchange with Piñera, see Thompson, ESPN.com.

p. 56 For "the life support," see *Diálogo* (June 11, 2010).

pp. 57–58 For "Can you imagine," see Jonathan Franklin and Mark Tran, *Guardian* (August 24, 2010).

p. 58 For "I haven't stopped," see Gregory, *Mirror* (August 26, 2010); for "Hello, my love" and "We never wrote," see Cristina Nunez, Maggie Nunez, et al, "Letters of Love, Carried by 'Doves' to Chilean Miners," interview by Annie Murphy, August 28, 2010, NPR News.

p. 59 For "This was more than," see Alexei Barrionuevo, *New York Times* (August 24, 2010).

CHAPTER NINE

p. 62 For "Raise borers," see Chavez, interview.

p. 64 For "We will hit," see Yang, *Toronto Star* (October 10, 2010).

p. 66 For "You're sleep-deprived," "you're in a risky," see Mary Roach, *Packing for Mars*, pages 49 and 50. Written for adults who read nonfiction for pleasure, this is accessible and well researched. The author has a lively, curious mind, and looks for answers to questions many people have but don't speak out loud—such as body odor in space. In that vein she investigates what we know about intimate relations between adults in space. Depending on the reader, that will make this book especially interesting or especially inappropriate.

p. 66 For "the same language," see *Diálogo* (June 11, 2010); for "put together a team," see *Diálogo* (November 4, 2010).

p. 66 For Dr. Al Holland's insights on group behavior, see Dr. Holland, interview by author (December 2010).

p. 67 Clint Cragg memo courtesy NASA.

CHAPTER TEN

p. 70 For "I ran to forget," see Wayne Coffey, *Daily News* (November 3, 2010); for "I was saying," see Liz Robbins, *New York Times* (November 4, 2010).

p. 70 For more on Dr. Duncan's exchange with miners, see Dr. Michael Duncan interview, "NASA Doc Details Chilean Miners Rescue," YouTube, youtube.com/watch?v=RkXN964rQb4.

p. **71** For "remain united and together," see Randy Woods and Matt Craze, *Bloomberg* (September 3, 2010); for "give away," see Alexei Barrionuevo and Simon Romero, *New York Times* (October 24, 2010).

p. **71** For "To Franklin Lobos," see Wright, ESPN.com.

p. **72** For the mood of the families, Holland, interview.

p. **74** For more of the families' journal entries, see *BBC News* (September 28, 2010).

CHAPTER ELEVEN

p. **75** For hearing the report on the way to church, Julie Fisher, interview by author (December 14, 2010); for "I don't know," WTAE Pittsburgh (October 11, 2010).

p. **75** For "well, heck," see Joe Mandak, Associated Press (October 13, 2010).

p. **76** For Fisher's use of state representatives, see Brandon Fisher, interview by author (December 2010).

p. **77** For "glorified jackhammer," see Yang, *Toronto Star* (October 10, 2010).

p. **78** For "long shot" and "the extreme," see *Sudbury Mining Solutions Journal* (December 2010).

p. **80** For "Obviously our interest," see AWWA Streamlines, vol. 2, no. 26 (November 2, 2010).

p. **82** For the timeline of Hart's arrival at the mine, especially as it related to the broken drill, see Brandon Fisher and Jeff Hart, interviews by author (February 2011).

p. 83 For the route from Afghanistan to Chile and "everything we do," Jeff Hart, interview by author (December 2010); for "We went back to basic math," see AWWA Streamlines (November 2, 2010).

p. 83 For "Mother, sister," see Fisher, interview.

p. 84 For "When are you going," see Yang, *Toronto Star* (October 10, 2010).

p. 86 For "went down to," see Julie Fisher, interview by author (December 2010).

CHAPTER TWELVE

p. 87 For more on Dr. Levine's role in assisting the miners, see UT Southwestern Medical Center's article (October 18, 2010).

AFTERWORD

p. 93 For "We are caught," see Martin Luther King Jr., "Letter from a Birmingham Jail" (April 1963).

BIBLIOGRAPHY

Franklin, Jonathan. *33 Men: Inside the Miraculous Survival and Dramatic Rescue of the Chilean Miners* (New York: G. P. Putnam's Sons, 2011).

Kristiansen, Kristian, and Thomas B. Larsson. *The Rise of Bronze Age Society* (Cambridge, England: Cambridge University Press, 2005).

Lamb, Simon. *Devil in the Mountain* (Princeton, NJ: Princeton University Press, 2004).

Lynch, Martin. *Mining in World History* (London, Reaktion Books, 2002).

Riordan, Rick. *The Lightning Thief* (New York: Scholastic, 2005).

Roach, Mary. *Packing for Mars* (New York: W.W. Norton, 2010).

Tafoya, Onofre, *Mother Magma* (Mesa, AZ: Hispanic Institute of Social Issues, 2006).

INTERVIEWS

(All interviews conducted December 2010)

Kelvin Brown

Dr. William Chavez

Brandon Fisher

Julie Fisher

Jeff Hart

Dr. Albert Holland

Ron Mishkin

USEFUL WEBSITES

Jennifer Yang, "From Collapse to Rescue, Inside the Chile Mine Disaster," *Toronto Star*, thestar.com/news/world/chile/article/873382

Fernando Barra, Robert Fromm, and Victor Valencia, "The Andes," geo.arizona.edu/geo5xx/geo527/Andes/intro.html

geo.arizona.edu/geo5xx/geo527/Andes/Magmandes.html

Clive Maund, "The Real Copiapó, The Real Atacama—by a Resource Stock Analyst Who Lived There" news.goldseek.com/CliveMaund/1287072563.php

Franklin Briceno and Eva Verara, "Chile Miners: From World Fame to Humble Homes," Associated Press, cbsnews.com/stories/2010/10/17/world/main6966657.shtml

Andrew Gregory, "Wife of Trapped Chilean Miner Mario Gómez Speaks Out," mirror.co.uk/news/top-stories/2010/08/26/wife-of-trapped-chilean-miner-mario-gomez-speaks-out-115875-22514081

"Miners Trapped in Chile," *Pakistan Observer*, pakobserver.net/201008/07/detailnews.asp?id=45650

"Chile Mine Collapse Leaves 34 Trapped," *Irish Times*, irishtimes.com/newspaper/breaking/2010/0806/breaking2.html

"Workers Trapped in Chile Mine Collapse" in ABC News (Australian Broadcasting Company), abc.net.au/news/stories/2010/08/06/2976126.htm

Jonathan Franklin, "Chilean Miners' Families Pitch up at Camp Home," guardian.co.uk/world/2010/aug/25/chilean-miners-families-camp-hope

Alonso Soto, "New Cave-in Blocks Bid to Rescue Chile Miners," reuters.com/article/idUSTRE6761JF20100808

Graeme Culliford, "'Mine Hell Was Worse Than Dying,'" mirror.co.uk/news/top-stories/2010/10/17/mine-hell-was-worse-than-dyng-115875-22640311

"Chile Miners Rescue: Miner 33 Foreman Luis Urzúa Describes How They Survived," mirror.co.uk/news/top-stories/2010/10/14/chile-miners-rescue-miner-33-foreman-luis-urzua-describes-how-they-survived-115875-22633250

Jonathan Franklin, "Chilean Miners: Foreman Says Unity of Men Is Humbling," guardian.co.uk/world/2010/oct/12/chilean-miners-foreman-unity-humbling

"Chile Mine Rescue: Luis Urzúa Profile," telegraph.co.uk/news/worldnews/southamerica/chile/8063051/Chile-mine-rescue-Luis-Urzua-profile.html

Jonathan Franklin and Juan Forero, "In Weeks Before Rescuers Made Contact, Miners Struggled with Despair," washingtonpost.com/wp-dyn/content/article/2010/10/14/AR2010101407196.html

Jonathan Franklin and Rory Carroll, "Chile Miners: Rescued Foreman Luis Urzúa's First Interview," guardian.co.uk/world/2010/oct/14/chile-miner-luis-urzua-interview

Kathy Kristof, "Chilean Miners: Leadership Lessons from Luis Urzúa," moneywatch.bnet.com/saving-money/blog/devil-details/chilean-miners-leadership-lessons-from-luis-urzua/3142

Alonso Soto, "No Quick Rescue for Trapped Chile Miners: Minister,"
reuters.com/article/idUSTRE6771F820100808

CNN Wire Staff, "Anxious Families Settle in as They Wait for Trapped
Miners," articles.cnn.com/2010-08-31/world/chile.miners
.families_1_deep-underground-mine-rocks?_s=PM:WORLD

Alonso Soto, "Rescue Bid for Chile Miners Moves Slowly 4 Days On,"
in.reuters.com/article/idINIndia-50722720100809

"Miscalculated Drilling Further Delays Rescue of Chilean Miners,"
earthtimes.org/articles/news/338855,delays-rescue-chilean-miners
.html

Roser Toll, "Chilean Rescuers Drill to Resupply Trapped Miners,"
Agence France Press, google.com/hostednews/afp/article/
ALeqM5ietkdUNDgSyoGyjaSnHtitnlzw9w

Rory Carroll, "Chilean Miners: Rival Churches Claim Credit for the
Miracle," guardian.co.uk/world/2010/oct/11/chilean-miners-rival
-churches-tussle

Wright Thompson, "Above and Beyond: The Story of a Former
Chilean Soccer Star's Survival in a Collapsed Mine and the
Love of a Town for a Team," sports.espn.go.com/espn/eticket/
story?page=101008/Chile

Jonathan Franklin and Juan Forero, "Chilean Miners to Begin
Emerging Tonight," washingtonpost.com/wp-dyn/content/
article/2010/10/12/AR2010101203510.html

Kelvin Brown, Lilian Gómez, Todd Russell, Brant Webb, Felipe
Silva, Mario Gómez, "Entombed," interview by Michael Usher,
September 10, 2010, transcript, *60 Minutes*, sixtyminutes.ninemsn
.com.au/article.aspx?id=7959384

Philip Sherwell, "Camp Hope Families Wait in Chile's Atacama Desert for Trapped Miners," telegraph.co.uk/news/worldnews/southamerica/chile/7969542/Camp-Hope-families-wait-in-Chiles-Atacama-Desert-for-trapped-miners.html

Simon Gardner and Terry Wade, "Chile's Miners Had Lost Hope, Prepared to Die," reuters.com/article/idUSTRE69I2M220101019

"WA's Chile Rescue Hero." *Stirling Times*, inmycommunity.com.au/news-and-views/local-news/WAs-Chile-rescue-hero/7572359/

"Sub Commander Kept Trapped Miners Healthy," dialogo-americas.com/en_GB/articles/rmisa/features/special_reports/2010/11/06/feature-01

Jonathan Franklin and Mark Tran, "Trapped Chilean Miners Start Receiving Food and Water," guardian.co.uk/world/2010/aug/24/trapped-chilean-miners-food-water

Cristina Nunez, Maggie [sic], Lily Pulgar, Chata Segovia, "Letters of Love, Carried by 'Doves' to Chilean Miners," interview by Annie Murphy, August 28, 2010, transcript, NPR News, npr.org/templates/story/story.php?storyId=129492507

Alexei Barrionuevo, "A Relieved Chile Braces for a Long Mine Rescue," nytimes.com/2010/08/25/world/americas/25chile.html?pagewanted=all

Wayne Coffey, "Chilean Miner No. 12 Edison Peña Tells Daily News How He Used Faith, Running to Reach NYC Marathon," nydailynews.com/sports/more_sports/2010/11/03/2010-11-03_chilean_miner_no_12_edison_pena_tells_daily_news_how_he_used_faith_running_to_re.html

Liz Robbins, "Ready for New York's Streets After Defying Death in Mine," nytimes.com/2010/11/05/sports/05miner.html

Dr. Michael Duncan interview, "NASA Doc Details Chilean Miners Rescue," YouTube, youtube.com/watch?v=RkXN964rQb4

Randy Woods and Matt Craze, "Chile Miners to Get Advice from 'Alive' Survivors," bloomberg.com/news/2010-09-03/chile-s -pinera-prepares-oil-drill-to-rescue-miners-update1 -.html?cmpid=yhoo

Alexei Barrionuevo and Simon Romero, "Stories of Hope and Hardship of 'Los 33,'" nytimes.com/2010/10/25/world/ americas/25chile.html?pagewanted=all

"Chile Miners: Family's Diary—September," bbc.co.uk/news/world -latin-america-11136021

"'It Was Unbelievable': Drill Bit Makers Return from Chile Rescue," wtae.com/r/25360492/detail.html

Joe Mandak, "Pa. Drill Firm Basking in Glow of Chilean Rescue," msnbc.msn.com/id/39656218/ns/business-us_business

"Sudbury, North Bay Companies Joined Chilean Mine Rescue," sudburyminingsolutions.com/articles/News/12-10-chilean-mine -rescue.asp

"AWWA Member Company Called to Free Miners in Chile," AWWA Streamlines, vol. 2, no. 26, awwa.org/publications/ StreamlinesArticle.cfm?itemnumber=55428

"UT Southwestern Doctor's Expertise Helped Trapped Chilean Miners During Pressured Half-Mile-Deep Rescue," utsouthwestern.edu/ utsw/cda/dept353744/files/612308.html

ACKNOWLEDGMENTS

Thanks to Namrata Tripathi and the crew at Simon & Schuster for asking me to do the impossible and to Jeannie Ng for keeping us all moving together and on pace. Once I began on that mad quest I was overwhelmed by the generosity of everyone I approached, especially my guides to mining: Ron Mishkin (everyone who can get to the Sterling Mine Museum in Ogdensburg, New Jersey, should go—ask for Ron) and Dr. William Chavez—who answered emails from a stranger with grace and deep knowledge. Special thanks to Claude Mound in Chile for sharing images and insight and to Earl Verbeek for venturing into the cold and wet Sterling mine to take photos of Ron and me. The state geologist of Nevada, whose name I did not catch, suggested I begin with the Sterling Mine, and he was so right. Thanks to Adrienne Mayor, Dr. William Hansen and Dr. Lora Holland for insights into Hephaistos.

This book literally could not exist without the extraordinary openness of the men and women who refuse to call themselves heroes but worked tirelessly to save the miners: Kelvin Brown, Brandon and Julie Fisher, Dr. Albert Holland, and Jeff Hart—all of whom were ready to share their stories with young readers and all of whom were patient with my steep learning-curve. This book is also a testament to the midnight oil efforts of our resourceful assistant, Chris Lynch, first as a William Paterson University intern then as a true team member, and of course my book-making partners, John W. Glenn of Aronson & Glenn, and Jon Glick of mouse+tiger. If there are blood brothers in gangs, there should be print brothers in books—for those who really do believe the best work comes when there is no limit to what every team member will do to get the book just right, on time, and in (generally) good spirits. Thanks, too, to Ken Wright for stitching together the agreements we all needed.

INDEX

Italic page numbers indicate illustrations or photographs.